Penguin Modern Poets
VOLUME 5

Simon Armitage was born in 1963 and lives in Huddersfield. His collections include *Zoom!* (1989), *Xanadu* (1992), *Kid* (1992) and *Book of Matches* (1993). In 1988 he was a recipient of an Eric Gregory award, in 1992 a winner of one of the first Forward Poetry Prizes, in 1993 he was the *Sunday Times* Writer of the Year, and in 1994 he received a Lannan Award. He is now poetry editor for Chatto & Windus and presents *Stanza*, BBC Radio 4's contemporary poetry programme. A new volume, *The Dead Sea Poems*, is due to be published in 1995.

Sean O'Brien was born in 1952, grew up in Hull, and read English at Cambridge. His collections to date are *The Indoor Park* (Bloodaxe, 1983; 1993), *The Frighteners* (Bloodaxe, 1987) and *HMS Glasshouse* (OUP, 1991). He has received the Somerset Maugham, Cholmondeley and E. M. Forster awards for his work. He is currently preparing *The Deregulated Muse*, a collection of essays on contemporary poetry, and his new book of poems, *Ghost Train*, is due to be published later in 1995. He is a reviewer and an editor of *The Printer's Devil*, and lives in Newcastle-upon-Tyne.

Tony Harrison was born in Leeds in 1937. His volumes of poetry include *The Loiners* (winner of the Geoffrey Faber Memorial Prize), *Continuous, v.* (broadcast on Channel 4 in 1987, winning the Royal Television Society Award) and *The Gaze of the Gorgon* (winner of the Whitbread Prize for Poetry). Recognized as Britain's leading theatre and film poet, Tony Harrison has written extensively for the National Theatre, the New York Metropolitan Opera, the BBC, Channel 4, and for unique ancient spaces in Greece and Austria. His *Theatre Works 1973–1985* are published by Penguin and his most recent theatre works, *The Tr........* and *The Common Chorus*, by Fab........ *........ Bride* won the Prix Italia in .... *........ Film Poems* is published in 1........

The Penguin Modern Poets Series

Volume One
James Fenton
Blake Morrison
Kit Wright

Volume Two
Carol Ann Duffy
Vicki Feaver
Eavan Boland

Volume Three
Glyn Maxwell
Mick Imlah
Peter Reading

Volume Four
Liz Lochhead
Roger McGough
Sharon Olds

Volume Five
Simon Armitage
Sean O'Brien
Tony Harrison

Penguin Modern Poets

VOLUME 5

SIMON ARMITAGE

SEAN O'BRIEN

TONY HARRISON

PENGUIN BOOKS

Published by the Penguin Group
Penguin Books Ltd, 27 Wrights Lane, London w8 5tz, England
Penguin Books USA Inc., 375 Hudson Street, New York, New York 10014, USA
Penguin Books Australia Ltd, Ringwood, Victoria, Australia
Penguin Books Canada Ltd, 10 Alcorn Avenue, Toronto, Ontario, Canada, m4v 3b2
Penguin Books (NZ) Ltd, 182–190 Wairau Road, Auckland 10, New Zealand

Penguin Books Ltd, Registered Offices: Harmondsworth, Middlesex, England

This selection first published 1995
10 9 8 7 6 5 4 3 2

Filmset by Datix International Limited, Bungay, Suffolk
Printed in England by Clays Ltd, St Ives plc
Set in Monophoto Garamond

Contents

Sean O'Brien

Tony Harrison

Simon Armitage

Snow Joke

Heard the one about the guy from Heaton Mersey?
Wife at home, lover in Hyde, mistress
in Newton-le-Willows and two pretty girls
in the top grade at Werneth prep. Well,

he was late and he had a good car so he snubbed
the police warning-light and tried to finesse
the last six miles of moorland blizzard,
and the story goes he was stuck within minutes.

So he sat there thinking about life and things;
what the dog does when it catches its tail
and about the snake that ate itself to death.
And he watched the windscreen filling up

with snow, and it felt good, and the whisky
from his hip-flask was warm and smooth.
And of course, there isn't a punchline
but the ending goes something like this.

They found him slumped against the steering wheel
with VOLVO printed backwards in his frozen brow.
And they fought in the pub over hot toddies
as to who was to take the most credit.

Him who took the aerial to be a hawthorn twig?
Him who figured out the contour of his car?
Or him who said he heard the horn, moaning
softly like an alarm clock under an eiderdown?

It Ain't What You Do It's What It Does To You

I have not bummed across America
with only a dollar to spare, one pair
of busted Levi's and a bowie knife.
I have lived with thieves in Manchester.

I have not padded through the Taj Mahal,
barefoot, listening to the space between
each footfall picking up and putting down
its print against the marble floor. But I

skimmed flat stones across Black Moss on a day
so still I could hear each set of ripples
as they crossed. I felt each stone's inertia
spend itself against the water; then sink.

I have not toyed with a parachute chord
while perched on the lip of a light-aircraft;
but I held the wobbly head of a boy
at the day centre, and stroked his fat hands.

And I guess that the tightness in the throat
and the tiny cascading sensation
somewhere inside us are both part of that
sense of something else. That feeling, I mean.

Poem

Frank O'Hara was open on the desk
but I went straight for the directory.
Nick was out, Joey was engaged, Jim was
just making coffee and why didn't I

come over. I had Astrud Gilberto
singing 'Bim Bom' on my Sony Walkman
and the sun was drying the damp slates on
the rooftops. I walked in without ringing

and he still wasn't dressed or shaved when we
topped up the coffee with his old man's scotch
(it was only half ten but what the hell)
and took the newspapers into the porch.

Talking Heads were on the radio. I
was just about to mention the football
when he said, 'Look, will you help me clear her
wardrobe out?' I said, 'Sure Jim, anything.'

A Painted Bird for Thomas Szasz

It was his anorak that first attracted me.
The foam lining was hanging from a split seam
and a tear that ran the length of his back was patched
with sellotape and sticking plaster. So I watched
as he flitted between the front seats of the bus
and fingered the synthetic fur around his hood.

The next time I noticed was at the terminus
where he was pretending to direct the buses.
From then there was a catalogue of incidents,
moments and locations where we coincided,
and each time I watched him talking to the drivers,
who ignored him, and jotting down the route numbers.

One particular time he was in the arcade
eyeing the intricacy of a timetable.
He caught me watching the reflection of his face
so he exhaled onto the surface of the glass
and wrote his name on it. Billy. I passed by him,
breathing in, and he smelt like a wet dog, drying.

Another time I noticed more than I meant to
was a lunchtime at the Probation Day Centre
where I squinted through the gap in the serving hatch
to see him watching the traffic on the bypass.
His focus settled on a simple bicycle
which he followed till it slipped below the skyline.

I also saw him, once, in the covered precinct
pissing himself through his pants onto the concrete
and fumbling with the zip on his anorak.
He bothered me, and later I had to walk back
across where the dark circle of his stain had grown
and was still growing, slowly, outward, like a town.

November

We walk to the ward from the badly parked car
with your grandma taking four short steps to our two.
We have brought her here to die and we know it.

You check her towel, soap and family trinkets,
pare her nails, parcel her in the rough blankets
and she sinks down into her incontinence.

It is time John. In their pasty bloodless smiles,
in their slack breasts, their stunned brains and their baldness,
and in us John: we are almost these monsters.

You're shattered. You give me the keys and I drive
through the twilight zone, past the famous station
to your house, to numb ourselves with alcohol.

Inside, we feel the terror of dusk begin.
Outside we watch the evening, failing again,
and we let it happen. We can say nothing.

Sometimes the sun spangles and we feel alive.
One thing we have to get, John, out of this life.

The Civilians

We signed the lease and knew we were landed.
Our dream house: half farm, half mansion; gardens
announcing every approach, a greenhouse
                              with a southern aspect.
                              Here the sunlight lasted;
evenings stretched their sunburnt arms towards us,
held us in their palms: gilded us, warmed us.

We studied the view as if we owned it;
noted each change, nodded and condoned it.
We rode with the roof down, and if the days
                              overstepped themselves
                              then the golden evenings
spread like ointment through the open valleys,
buttered one side of our spotless washing.

Forget the dangers of iron pyrites
or the boy who ran from his mother's farm
to the golden house on the other hill
                              which was a pigsty
                              taking the sunlight.
This was God's glory. The big wheel had stopped
with our chair rocking sweetly at the summit.

For what we have, or had, we are grateful.
                              To say otherwise
                              would be bitterness
and we know better than to surrender.
Behind the hen-house the jalopy is snookered:
                              its bodywork sound,
                              its engine buggered,
but still there is gold: headlights on the road,

the unchewable crusts of our own loaves,
                          old leaves the dog drags in.
                          Frost is early this autumn.
                          Wrapped up like onions
we shuffle out over the frozen ground;
prop up the line where our sheets are flagging.

The Stuff

We'd heard all the warnings; knew its nicknames.
It arrived in our town by word of mouth
and crackled like wildfire through the grapevine
of gab and gossip. It came from the south

        so we shunned it, naturally;
        sent it to Coventry

and wouldn't have touched it with a barge pole
if it hadn't been at the club one night.
Well, peer group pressure and all that twaddle
so we fussed around it like flies round shite

        and watched,
        and waited

till one kid risked it, stepped up and licked it
and came from every pore in his body.
That clinched it. It snowballed; whirlpooled. Listen,
no one was more surprised than me to be

        cutting it, mixing it,
        snorting and sniffing it

or bulking it up with scouring powder
or chalk, or snuff, or sodium chloride
and selling it under the flyover.
At first we were laughing. It was alright

        to be drinking it, eating it,
        living and breathing it

but things got seedy; people went missing.
One punter surfaced in the ship-canal
having shed a pair of concrete slippers.
Others were bundled in the back of vans

and were quizzed, thumped,
finished off and dumped

or vanished completely like Weldon Kees:
their cars left idle under the rail bridge
with its cryptic hoarding which stumped the police:
'Oldham – Home of the tubular bandage.'

Others were strangled.
Not that it stopped us.

Someone bubbled us. CID sussed us
and found some on us. It was cut and dried.
They dusted, booked us, cuffed us and pushed us
down to the station and read us our rights.

Possession and supplying:
we had it, we'd had it.

In Court I ambled up and took the oath
and spoke the addict's side of the story.
I said grapevine, barge pole, whirlpool, chloride,
concrete, bandage, station, story. Honest.

B & B

It's easier than falling off a log.
Down south they call it doing a runner
but for us it is an art form of course.
Swanning round the foothills of The Cobbler
we are model tourists in every way:
keeping to the paths, following the code,
upbraiding litterlouts at every turn.
And then the dead mole: soft as a pocket,
perfect like a small velvet purse whose snout
we might unclasp and silver down inside:
money enough for tonight's feast. The soup
at the side of the bowl is coolest.

Nothing as cheap as an open window
or shinning down a drainpipe at midnight
or down paying a suitcase full of bricks.
To our hosts we are almost cousinly
who pity my grasp of their mother tongue.
This morning I was the stupid Polack
fetching his O.S. map from the camper,
but as they sketched a foolproof route for Ayr
we were sashaying all the way to Largs
with a fortnight's free board under our belt
and two packed lunches for the trip. A smile,
after all, is two sneers on the same lip.

The Monday had been a proper scorcher.
After readjusting the number plates
and lapping heather into the front grille
we set down in a passing-place and basked
in our finest hour. Promising fresh trout
for breakfast we had risen with the lark

and to this day she will swear us both drowned.
It was dark. The wall was down. Arm in arm
along the bank with slow dégagé steps
we had seen the cordon as a handrail;
shown ourselves into the river. The sun,
not the storm, will remove a man's blazer.

Zoom!

It begins as a house, an end terrace
in this case
    but it will not stop there. Soon it is
an avenue
    which cambers arrogantly past the Mechanics' Institute,
turns left
    at the main road without even looking
and quickly it is
    a town with all four major clearing banks,
a daily paper
    and a football team pushing for promotion.

On it goes, oblivious of the Planning Acts,
the green belts,
    and before we know it it is out of our hands:
city, nation,
    hemisphere, universe, hammering out in all directions
until suddenly,
    mercifully, it is drawn aside through the eye
of a black hole
    and bulleted into a neighbouring galaxy, emerging
smaller and smoother
    than a billiard ball but weighing more than Saturn.

People stop me in the street, badger me
in the check-out queue
    and ask, 'What is this, this that is so small
and so very smooth
    but whose mass is greater than the ringed planet?'
It's just words
    I assure them. But they will not have it.

Brassneck

United, mainly,
every odd Saturday,
or White Hart Lane for a worthwhile away game.
Down in the crowds at the grounds where the bread is:
the gold, the plastic,
the cheque-books, the readies,

the biggest fish
or the easiest meat,
or both. Consider that chap we took last week:
we turned him over and walked off the terrace
with a grand exactly
in dog-eared tenners;

takings like that
don't get reported.
Carter, he's a sort of junior partner;
it's two seasons now since we first teamed up
in the Stretford End
in the FA Cup;

it was all United
when I caught him filching
my cigarette case, and he felt me fishing
a prial of credit cards out of his britches.
Since that day
we've worked these pitches.

We tend to kick off
by the hot dog vans
and we've lightened a good many fair-weather fans
who haven't a clue where to queue for tickets.
Anything goes, if it's
loose we lift it.

At City last year
in the derby match
we did the right thing with a smart-looking lass
who'd come unhitched in the crush from her friend.
We escorted her out
of the Platt Lane End,

arm in arm
along the touchline,
past the tunnel and out through the turnstile
and directed her on to a distant police car.
I did the talking
and Carter fleeced her.

As Carter once put it:
when we're on the ball
we can clean someone out, from a comb to a coil,
and we need nine eyes to watch for the coppers
though at Goodison Park
when I got collared

two bright young bobbies
took me into the toilets
and we split the difference. Bent policemen;
there's always a couple around when you need them.
It's usually Autumn
when we loosen our fingers

at the Charity Shield
which is pretty big business
though semis and finals are birthdays and Christmas.
Hillsborough was a different ball game of course;
we'd started early,
then saw what the score was,

so we turned things in
as a mark of respect,
just kept enough back to meet certain expenses
(I'm referring here to a red and blue wreath;
there are trading standards,
even among thieves).

Carter keeps saying
he'd be quick to wager
that worse things go on in the name of wages,
but I've let Carter know there's a place and a time
to say as we speak,
speak as we find.

Speaking of Carter,
and not that I mind,
he thinks I'm a touch on the gingery side:
my voice a little too tongued and grooved,
my locks a little
too washed and groomed,
my cuticles tenderly
pushed back and pruned,
both thumbnails capped with a full half-moon,
each fingernail manicured, pared and polished . . .
We can work hand in hand if we stick to the rules:
he keeps his cunt-hooks out of my wallet,
I keep my tentacles
out of his pocket.

You May Turn Over and Begin . . .

'Which of these films was Dirk Bogarde
not in? One hundredweight of bauxite

makes how much aluminium?
How many tales in *The Decameron*?'

General Studies, the upper sixth, a doddle, a cinch
for anyone with an ounce of common sense

or a calculator
with a memory feature.

Having galloped through but not caring enough
to check or double-check, I was dreaming of

milk-white breasts and nakedness, or more specifically
virginity.

That term – everybody felt the heat
but the girls were having none of it:

long and cool like cocktails,
out of reach, their buns and pigtails

only let out for older guys with studded jackets
and motor-bikes and spare helmets.

One jot of consolation
was the tall spindly girl riding pillion

on her man's new Honda
who, with the lights at amber,

put down both feet and stood to stretch her limbs,
to lift the visor and push back her fringe

and to smooth her tight jeans.
As he pulled off down the street

she stood there like a wishbone,
high and dry, her legs wide open,

and rumour has it he didn't notice
till he came round in the ambulance

having underbalanced on a tight left-hander.
A Taste of Honey. Now I remember.

At Sea

It is not through weeping,
but all evening the pale blue eye
on your most photogenic side has kept
its own unfathomable tide. Like the boy
at the dyke I have been there:

held out a huge finger,
lifted atoms of dust with the point
of a tissue and imagined slivers of hair
in the oil on the cornea. We are both
in the dark, but I go on

drawing the eyelid up by its lashes,
folding it almost inside-out, then finding
and hiding every mirror in the house
as the iris, besieged with the ink
of blood rolls back

into its own orbit. Nothing
will help it. Through until dawn
you dream the true story of the boy
who hooked out his eye and ate it,
so by six in the morning

I am steadying the ointment
that will bite like an onion, piping
a line of cream while avoiding the pupil
and in no time it is glued shut
like a bad mussel.

Friends call round
and mean well. They wait
and whisper in the air-lock of the lobby
with patches, eyewash, the truth
about mascara.

Even the cats are on to it;
they bring in starlings, and because their feathers
are the colours of oil on water in sunlight
they are a sign of something.
In the long hours

beyond us, irritations heal
into arguments. For the eighteenth time
it comes to this: the length of your leg sliding out
from the covers, the ball of your foot
like a fist on the carpet

while downstairs
I cannot bring myself to hear it.
Words have been spoken; things that were bottled
have burst open and to walk in now
would be to walk in

on the ocean.

Poem

And if it snowed and snow covered the drive
he took a spade and tossed it to one side.
And always tucked his daughter up at night.
And slippered her the one time that she lied.

And every week he tipped up half his wage.
And what he didn't spend each week he saved.
And praised his wife for every meal she made.
And once, for laughing, punched her in the face.

And for his mum he hired a private nurse.
And every Sunday taxied her to church.
And he blubbed when she went from bad to worse.
And twice he lifted ten quid from her purse.

Here's how they rated him when they looked back:
sometimes he did this, sometimes he did that.

Kid

Batman, big shot, when you gave the order
to grow up, then let me loose to wander
leeward, freely through the wild blue yonder
as you liked to say, or ditched me, rather,
in the gutter . . . well, I turned the corner.
Now I've scotched that 'he was like a father
to me' rumour, sacked it, blown the cover
on that 'he was like an elder brother'
story, let the cat out on that caper
with the married woman, how you took her
downtown on expenses in the motor.
Holy robin-redbreast-nest-egg-shocker!
Holy roll-me-over-in-the-clover,
I'm not playing ball boy any longer
Batman, now I've doffed that off-the-shoulder
Sherwood-Forest-green and scarlet number
for a pair of jeans and crew-neck jumper;
now I'm taller, harder, stronger, older.
Batman, it makes a marvellous picture:
you without a shadow, stewing over
chicken giblets in the pressure cooker,
next to nothing in the walk-in larder,
punching the palm of your hand all winter,
you baby, now I'm the real boy wonder.

Great Sporting Moments: The Treble

The rich! I love them. Trust them to suppose
the gift of tennis is deep in their bones.

Those chaps from the coast with all their own gear
from electric eyes to the umpire's chair,

like him whose arse I whipped with five choice strokes
perfected on West Yorkshire's threadbare courts:

a big first serve that strained his alloy frame,
a straight return that went back like a train,

a lob that left him gawping like a fish,
a backhand pass that kicked and drew a wisp

of chalk, a smash like a rubber bullet
and a bruise to go with it. Three straight sets.

Smarting in the locker rooms he offered
double or quits; he was a born golfer

and round the links he'd wipe the floor with me.
I played the ignoramus to a tee:

the pleb in the gag who asked the viscount
what those eggcup-like things were all about –

'They're to rest my balls on when I'm driving.'
'Blimey, guv, Rolls-Royce think of everything' –

but at the fifth when I hadn't faltered
he lost his rag and threw down the gauntlet;

we'd settle this like men: with the gloves on.
I said no, no, no, no, no, no, no. OK, come on then.

Lines Thought to have been Written on the Eve of the Execution of a Warrant for His Arrest

Boys, I have a feeling in my water,
in my bones, that should we lose our houses
and our homes, our jobs, or just in general
come unstuck, she will not lend one button
from her blouse, and from her kitchen garden
not one bean. But through farmyards and dust bowls
we will lay down out topcoats, or steel ourselves
and bare our backs over streams and manholes.

Down Birdcage Walk in riots or wartime
we will not hear of her hitching her skirt
or see for ourselves that frantic footwork,
busy like a swan's beneath the surface.
But quickly our tank will stop in its tracks;
they'll turn the turret lid back like a stone;
inside, our faces set like flint, her name
cross-threaded in the barrels of our throats.

I have this from reliable sources:
boys, with our letters, our first-class honours
and diplomas we are tenfold brighter
than her sons and daughters put together.
But someone hangs on every word they speak,
and let me mention here the hummingbird
that seems suspended at the orchid's lips,
or else the bird that picks the hippo's teeth.

Boys, if we burn, she will not pass one drop
of water over us, and if we drown
she will not let a belt or bootlace down,
or lend a hand. She'll turn instead and show

a leg, a stocking, sheer and ladderless.
And even then we will not lose our heads
by mouthing an air bubble out of turn
or spouting a smoke ring against her name.

But worse than this, in handouts and speeches
she will care for us, and cannot mean it.
Picture the stroke of the hour that takes her:
our faces will freeze as if the wind had changed,
we shall hear in our hearts a note, a murmur,
and talk in terms of where we stood, how struck,
how still we were the moment this happened,
in good faith, as if it really mattered.

Not the Furniture Game

His hair was a crow fished out of a blocked chimney
and his eyes were boiled eggs with the tops hammered in
and his blink was a cat flap
and his teeth were bluestones or Easter Island statues
and his bite was a perfect horseshoe.
His nostrils were both barrels of a shotgun, loaded.
And his mouth was an oil exploration project gone bankrupt
and his last smile was a caesarean section
and his tongue was an iguanodon
and his whistle was a laser beam
and his laugh was a bad case of kennel cough.
He coughed, and it was malt whisky.
And his headaches were Arson in Her Majesty's Dockyards
and his arguments were outboard motors strangled with fishing-
    line
and his neck was a bandstand
and his Adam's apple was a ball cock
and his arms were milk running off from a broken bottle.
His elbows were boomerangs or pinking shears.
And his wrists were ankles
and his handshakes were puff adders in the bran tub
and his fingers were astronauts found dead in their spacesuits
and the palms of his hands were action paintings
and both thumbs were blue touchpaper.
And his shadow was an opencast mine.
And his dog was a sentry-box with no one in it
and his heart was a first world war grenade discovered by
    children
and his nipples were timers for incendiary devices
and his shoulder-blades were two butchers at the meat-cleaving
    competition

and his belly-button was the Falkland Islands
and his private parts were the Bermuda triangle
and his backside was a priest hole
and his stretchmarks were the tide going out.
The whole system of his blood was Dutch elm disease.
And his legs were depth charges
and his knees were fossils waiting to be tapped open
and his ligaments were rifles wrapped in oilcloth under the
    floorboards
and his calves were the undercarriages of Shackletons.
The balls of his feet were where meteorites had landed
and his toes were a nest of mice under the lawn-mower.
And his footprints were Vietnam
and his promises were hot-air balloons floating off over the
    trees
and his one-liners were footballs through other people's
    windows
and his grin was the Great Wall of China as seen from the moon
and the last time they talked, it was apartheid.

She was a chair, tipped over backwards
with his donkey jacket on her shoulders.

They told him,
and his face was a hole
where the ice had not been thick enough to hold her.

Robinson's Resignation

Because I am done with this thing called work,
the paper-clips and staples of it all.
The customers and their huge excuses,
their incredulous lies and their beautiful
foul-mouthed daughters. I am swimming with it,
right up to here with it. And I am bored,
bored like the man who married a mermaid.

And I am through with the business of work.
In meetings, with the minutes, I have dreamed
and doodled, drifted away then undressed
and dressed almost every single woman,
every button, every zip and buckle.
For eighteen months in this diving-helmet
I have lived with the stench of my own breath.

So I am finished with the whole affair.
As for this friendship thing, I couldn't give
a weeping fig for those so-called brothers
who are all voltage, no current. I have
emptied my locker. I should like to leave
and to fold things now like a pair of gloves
or two clean socks, one into the other.

This is my final word. Nothing will follow.

About His Person

Five pounds fifty in change, exactly,
a library card on its date of expiry.

A postcard, stamped,
unwritten, but franked,

a pocket-size diary slashed with a pencil
from March twenty-fourth to the first of April.

A brace of keys for a mortise lock,
an analogue watch, self-winding, stopped.

A final demand
in his own hand,

a rolled-up note of explanation
planted there like a spray carnation

but beheaded, in his fist.
A shopping list.

A giveaway photograph stashed in his wallet,
a keepsake banked in the heart of a locket.

No gold or silver,
but crowning one finger

a ring of white unweathered skin.
That was everything.

Map Reference

Not that it was the first peak in the range,
or the furthest.
It didn't have the swankiest name
and wasn't the highest even, or the finest.

In fact, if those in the know
ever had their say about sea-level or cross-sections,
or had their way with angles and vectors,
or went there with their instruments about them,
it might have been more of a hill than a mountain.

As for its features,
walls fell into stones along its lower reaches,
fields ran up against its footslopes, scree had loosened
from around its shoulders. Incidentally, pine trees
pitched about its south and west approaches.

We could have guessed, I think, had we taken to it,
the view, straightforward, from its summit.

So,
as we rounded on it from the road that day,
how very smart of me to say or not to say
what we both knew:
that it stood where it stood, so absolutely, for you.

The Lost Letter of the Late Jud Fry

Wake.
And in my head
walk barefoot, naked from the bed
towards the day, then
wait.

Hold.
The dawn will crack
its egg into the morning's bowl
and him on horseback,
gold.

Me,
I'm in the shed, I'm
working on it: a plus b plus c, it's
you, him, me. It's
three.

Hell,
this hole, this shack.
The sun makes light of me
behind my back.
Well,

good.
I give you the applause
of ringdoves lifting from the wood
and, for an encore,
blood.

Look,
see, no man
should be me, the very opposite
of snowman:
soot.

I
work that black dust
where I slice your name into my forearm
with a jackknife: L.A.U.R.E
Y.

You,
at the window now,
undressed. I underestimated him,
never saw you as a pair, a
two.

Yours –
that's him for sure.
The sun will have its day,
its weeks, months,
years.

Fine.
But just for once, for me,
dig deep, think twice, be otherwise, be
someone else this time.
Mine.

To Poverty

After Laycock

You are near again, and have been there
or thereabouts for years. Pull up a chair.
I'd know that shadow anywhere, that silhouette
without a face, that shape. Well, be my guest.
We'll live like sidekicks – hip to hip,
like Siamese twins, joined at the pocket.

I've tried too long to see the back of you.
Last winter when you came down with the flu
I should have split, cut loose, but
let you pass the buck, the bug. Bad blood.
It's cold again; come closer to the fire, the light,
and let me make you out.

How have you hurt me, let me count the ways:
the months of Sundays
when you left me in the damp, the dark,
the red, or down and out, or out of work.
The weeks on end of bread without butter,
bed without supper.

That time I fell through Schofield's shed
and broke both legs,
and Schofield couldn't spare to split
one stick of furniture to make a splint.
Thirteen weeks I sat there till they set.
What can the poor do but wait? And wait.

How come you're struck with me? Go see the Queen,
lean on the doctor or the dean,
breathe on the major,
squeeze the mason or the manager,
go down to London, find a novelist at least
to bother with, to bleed, to leech.

On second thoughts, stay put.
A person needs to get a person close enough
to stab him in the back.
Robert Frost said that. Besides,
I'd rather keep you in the corner of my eye
than wait for you to join me side by side
at every turn, on every street, in every town.
Sit down. I said sit down.

You

hold the page out like a work of art,
see for yourself, comb through it twice, three times,
look for your likeness in the lines but find
someone else.

When did I ever see you wear a hat?
You certainly never said that. Or that.
Fiction, I say. You take the page again,
catch the light,

see through it once, then twice, then strike a match.
I am a cheat, a bastard, and a liar.
You tear it into two, four, eight, sixteen,
feed the fire.

Parable of the Dead Donkey

Instructions arrived by registered post
under cover of separate envelopes:
directions first
to pinpoint the place
in the shape of maps and compass bearings;
those, then forms and stamps for loss of earnings.
So much was paid
to diggers of graves
by keepers or next of kin, per leg
(which made for the dumping of quadrupeds):
sixteen quid
to send off a pig
or sink a pit for a dog or pony.
But less to plant a man than a donkey.
Cheaper by half
for a pregnant horse
that died with all four hooves inside her
than one with a stillborn foal beside her.
And this was a bind,
being duty bound
where ownership was unestablished.
We filled the flasks and loaded the Transit,
then set out, making
for the undertaking.

Facing north, he was dead at three o'clock
in a ring of meadow grass, closely cropped,
where a metal chain
on a wooden stake
had stopped him ambling off at an angle,
worn him down in a perfect circle.
We burrowed in
right next to him
through firm white soil. An hour's hard labour
took us five feet down – and then the weather:

thunder biting
the heels of lightning,
a cloudburst drawing a curtain of rain
across us, filling the bath of the grave,
and we waded in it
for one more minute,
dredged and shovelled as the tide was rising,
bailed out for fear of drowning, capsizing.
Back on top
we weighed him up,
gave some thought to this beast of the Bible:
the nose and muzzle, the teeth, the eyeballs,
the rump, the hindquarters,
the flanks, the shoulders,
everything soothed in the oil of the rain –
the eel of his tongue, the keel of his spine,
the rope of his tail,
the weeds of his mane.
Then we turned him about and slipped his anchor,
eased him out of the noose of his tether,
and rolled him in
and started to dig.
But even with donkey, water and soil
there wasn't enough to level the hole
after what was washed away
or turned into clay
or trodden in, so we opened the earth
and started in on a second trench for dirt
to fill the first.
Which left a taste
of starting something that wouldn't finish:
a covered grave with a donkey in it,
a donkey-size hole
within a stone's throw
and not a single bone to drop in it
or a handful of dust to toss on top of it.

The van wouldn't start, so we wandered home
on foot, in the dark, without supper or profit.

Hitcher

I'd been tired, under
the weather, but the ansaphone kept screaming:
One more sick-note, mister, and you're finished. Fired.
I thumbed a lift to where the car was parked.
A Vauxhall Astra. It was hired.

I picked him up in Leeds.
He was following the sun to west from east
with just a toothbrush and the good earth for a bed. The truth,
he said, was blowin' in the wind,
or round the next bend.

I let him have it
on the top road out of Harrogate – once
with the head, then six times with a krooklok
in the face – and didn't even swerve.
I dropped it into third

and leant across
to let him out, and saw him in the mirror
bouncing off the kerb, then disappearing down the verge.
We were the same age, give or take a week.
He'd said he liked the breeze

to run its fingers
through his hair. It was twelve noon.
The outlook for the day was moderate to fair.
Stitch that, I remember thinking,
you can walk from there.

To His Lost Lover

Now they are no longer
any trouble to each other

he can turn things over, get down to that list
of things that never happened, all of the lost

unfinishable business.
For instance . . . for instance,

how he never clipped and kept her hair, or drew a hairbrush
through that style of hers, and never knew how not to blush

at the fall of her name in close company.
How they never slept like buried cutlery –

two spoons or forks cupped perfectly together,
or made the most of some heavy weather –

walked out into hard rain under sheet lightning,
or did the gears while the other was driving.

How he never raised his fingertips
to stop the segments of her lips

from breaking the news,
or tasted the fruit,

or picked for himself the pear of her heart,
or lifted her hand to where his own heart

was a small, dark, terrified bird
in her grip. Where it hurt.

Or said the right thing,
or put it in writing.

And never fled the black mile back to his house
before midnight, or coaxed another button of her blouse,

then another,
or knew her

favourite colour,
her taste, her flavour,

and never ran a bath or held a towel for her,
or soft-soaped her, or whipped her hair

into an ice-cream cornet or a beehive
of lather, or acted out of turn, or misbehaved

when he might have, or worked a comb
where no comb had been, or walked back home

through a black mile hugging a punctured heart,
where it hurt, where it hurt, or helped her hand

to his butterfly heart
in its two blue halves.

And never almost cried,
and never once described

an attack of the heart,
or under a silk shirt

nursed in his hand her breast,
her left, like a tear of flesh

wept by the heart,
where it hurts,

or brushed with his thumb the nut of her nipple,
or drank intoxicating liquors from her navel.

Or christened the Pole Star in her name,
or shielded the mask of her face like a flame,

a pilot light,
or stayed the night,

or steered her back to that house of his,
or said, 'Don't ask me to say how it is

I like you.
I just might do.'

How he never figured out a fireproof plan,
or unravelled her hand, as if her hand

were a solid ball
of silver foil

and discovered a lifeline hiding inside it,
and measured the trace of his own alongside it.

But said some things and never meant them —
sweet nothings anybody could have mentioned.

And left unsaid some things he should have spoken,
about the heart, where it hurt exactly, and how often.

Becoming of Age

The year the institutions would not hold.
The autumn when the convicts took their leave.
The month the radio went haywire, gargled
through the long-range forecast, and their names.
The fortnight of the curfew, and the cheese-wire
of the Klaxon slicing day from night, night
from day. The clear, unclouded ocean

of the sky. The week we met. The afternoon
we might have seen a ghost, a scarecrow
striding boldly down The Great North Road
towards us, wearing everything he owned.

The minute in the phone box with the coin,
the dialling tone, the disagreement – heads
to turn him in to the authorities, or tails
to leave him be, to let him go to ground
and keep the public footpaths trodden down,
the green lanes and the bridleways.

Then on the glass, each in its own time – one,
two, three, four, five, six fingerprints of rain.

from BOOK OF MATCHES

My party piece:
I strike, then from the moment when the matchstick
conjures up its light, to when the brightness moves
beyond its means, and dies, I say the story
of my life –

dates and places, torches I carried,
a cast of names and faces, those
who showed me love, or came close,
the changes I made, the lessons I learnt –

then somehow still find time to stall and blush
before I'm bitten by the flame, and burnt.

A warning, though, to anyone nursing
an ounce of sadness, anyone alone:
don't try this on your own; it's dangerous,
madness.

★

Strike two. My mind works
quickly and well these days,
and I like the look of myself of late:

a little more meat
around the face, a little more bite
at the back of the lungs,
a little more point to the tip of the tongue –
no wonder I've been smiling
like a melon with a slice missing.

At twenty-eight
I'm not doing great,
but considering I came from the River Colne
and its long, lifeless mud,
I'm doing good.

★

Mother, any distance greater than a single span
requires a second pair of hands.
You come to help me measure windows, pelmets, doors,
the acres of the walls, the prairies of the floors.

You at the zero-end, me with the spool of tape, recording
length, reporting metres, centimetres back to base, then leaving
up the stairs, the line still feeding out, unreeling
years between us. Anchor. Kite.

I space-walk through the empty bedrooms, climb
the ladder to the loft, to breaking point, where something
has to give;
two floors below your fingertips still pinch
the last one-hundredth of an inch . . . I reach
towards a hatch that opens on an endless sky
to fall or fly.

★

My father thought it bloody queer,
the day I rolled home with a ring of silver in my ear
half hidden by a mop of hair. 'You've lost your head.
If that's how easily you're led
you should've had it through your nose instead.'

And even then I hadn't had the nerve to numb
the lobe with ice, then drive a needle through the skin,
then wear a safety-pin. It took a jeweller's gun
to pierce the flesh, and then a friend
to thread a sleeper in, and where it slept
the hole became a sore, became a wound, and wept.

At twenty-nine, it comes as no surprise to hear
my own voice breaking like a tear, released like water,
cried from way back in the spiral of the ear. *If I were you,*
I'd take it out and leave it out next year.

I am very bothered when I think
of the bad things I have done in my life.
Not least that time in the chemistry lab
when I held a pair of scissors by the blades
and played the handles
in the naked lilac flame of the Bunsen burner;
then called your name, and handed them over.

O the unrivalled stench of branded skin
as you slipped your thumb and middle finger in,
then couldn't shake off the two burning rings. Marked,
the doctor said, for eternity.

Don't believe me, please, if I say
that was just my butterfingered way, at thirteen,
of asking you if you would marry me.

A safe rule in life is: trust nobody.
That's the first, and secondly,
the man with 20/20 vision who achieves the peak
of Everest (forgetting for now the curve
of the Earth), looks east and west and gets
a perfect view of the back of his head.

Third, there will always be
that square half-inch or so of unscratchable skin
between the shoulder blades, unreachable
from over the top or underneath. And fourth,

as I once heard said, don't go inventing
the acid that will eat through anything
without giving some thought
to a jar to keep it in.

I live in fear of letting people down.
Last winter, someone leaked the blueprint for a plan
to put the town back on the map:
that everyone should stand and strike a match
at midnight on the shortest, darkest day,
then photograph it from an aeroplane. No way:

the workers wouldn't break bread with the upper class,
the wealthy wouldn't mingle with the mob,
the worthy knew a thing or two about sulphuric gas.

It came to pass that only one man struck; a man whose job
or game was civic unrest and civil dissent, but who claimed
to be lighting his pipe in any event,
a man whose face turned purple as he spoke.

I know very well that man doesn't smoke.

★

I'm dreaming of that work, *Man Seated Reading
at a Table in a Lofty Room*, and while I sleep
a virus sweeps the earth, and when I wake I see
the population of the world is

me.

I take the observation suite in Emley Moor Mast
to watch the skyline from the Appalachians to the Alps;
those signs of life, a thousand miles away perhaps,
are nothing more than fireflies nesting in the grass
across the fell.

I manage very well, become a master in the arts
of food and drink and heat and light,
but then at night, with no one in the world
to cut my throat, I lock and latch
and bar and bolt the windows and the hatch.

Brung up with swine, I was,
and dogs,
and raised on a diet of slime and slops
and pobs, then fell in one day
with a different kind. Some say

that gives me the right
to try out that line
about having a bark and having a bite,
and a nose for uncovering truffles, or shite.
Or, put another way,

what looks from afar
like a cloak of fur
is a coat of hair. Cut back the hair to find
not skin, but rind.

★

Those bastards in their mansions:
to hear them shriek, you'd think
I'd poisoned the dogs and vaulted the ditches,
crossed the lawns in stocking feet and threadbare britches,
forced the door of one of the porches, and lifted
the gift of fire from the burning torches,

then given heat and light to streets and houses,
told the people how to ditch their cuffs and shackles,
armed them with the iron from their wrists and ankles.

Those lords and ladies in their palaces and castles,
they'd have me sniffed out by their beagles,
picked at by their eagles, pinned down, grilled
beneath the sun.

Me, I stick to the shadows, carry a gun.

★

æŋkɪˈləʊzɪŋ spɒndɪˈlaɪtɪs:
ankylosing meaning bond or join,
and spondylitis meaning of the bone or spine.
That half explains the cracks and clicks,
the clockwork of my joints and discs,
the ratchet of my hips. I'm fossilizing –
every time I rest
I let the gristle knit, weave, mesh.

My dear, my skeleton will set like biscuit overnight,
like glass, like ice, and you can choose
to snap me back to life before first light,
or let me laze until
the shape I take becomes the shape I keep.

Don't leave me be. Don't let me sleep.

★

Let this matchstick be a brief biography,
the sign or symbol
for the lifetime of a certain someone.

How a spark of light
went to his head, but
how that halo soon came loose,
became a noose,
a girdle, then a belt, a Hula-Hoop
of inflammation spreading through his frame
to take his legs and black his boots,

and left him spent, bent
out of line,
a saint, burnt at the stake,
the spine.

48

I've made out a will; I'm leaving myself
to the National Health. I'm sure they can use
the jellies and tubes and syrups and glues,
the web of nerves and veins, the loaf of brains,
an assortment of fillings and stitches and wounds,
blood – a gallon exactly of bilberry soup –
the chassis or cage or cathedral of bone;
but not the heart, they can leave that alone.

They can have the lot, the whole stock:
the loops and coils and sprockets and springs and rods,
the twines and cords and strands,
the face, the case, the cogs and the hands,

but not the pendulum, the ticker;
leave that where it stops or hangs.

Life:
behind the spreading butter comes the knife;
the deaf and dumb and blind man dozing
in a field of rape, found by the sickle
or the scythe. I'd been supposing

that it all adds up
to something times the power
of infinity recurring, but

it doesn't take a flying pass
in Further Maths
to figure out the sum
of what's already gone, what's going on
and what's to come.
It's none.

★

No convictions – that's my one major fault.
Nothing to tempt me to scream and shout, nothing
to raise Cain or make a song and dance about.

A man like me could be a real handful,
steeping himself overnight in petrol,
becoming inflamed on behalf of the world,
letting his blood boil, letting his hair curl.

I have a beauty spot three inches south-east
of my nose, a heart that has to be a match
for any pocket watch, a fist
that opens like a fine Swiss Army knife,
and certain tricks that have been known
to bring about spontaneous applause.
But no cause, no cause.

★

Thinking back, they either pulled me like a tooth,
or drew me like a rabbit from a hat,
or else I came to life
like something frantic from under the ice

on Sunday the twenty-sixth of May
nineteen sixty-three.
It was thirteen hundred hours, GMT.

Whichever way, it's either passed me by
at something close to the speed of light,
or else I've lived it frame by frame, the whole
slow-motion picture show,
as if that day were thirty years, nine hours,
eleven minutes, five,
six, seven spasms of the second hand ago.

Sean O'Brien

The Snowfield

It is so simple, being lonely.
It's there in the silence you make
To deny it, the silence you make
To accuse the unwary, the frankly alone.
In the silence you bring to a park
When you go there to walk in the snow
And you find in the planthouse,
Next to the orchids in winter slow-motion
And sleeping unreadable mosses,
Sick men, mad, half-born, who are sitting
As long as the afternoon takes.
Left there by helpers hours ago,
As if preparing for a test,
Each holds a book he cannot open.

Some days you put together
Sentences to say for them
As you leave to go back to the street.
With work they might be epigrams
Of love and modest government.
And this thought frees you. You pick up the paper.
You eat. Or you go to the library and talk.

But some days there is nothing
You cannot know. You still leave,
But it seems to take hours, labouring
Back to the street through the snowdrifts
And not worth the effort.
It seems that this is all there is.
It happens like snow in a park, seen clearly
After days of admiration, and looking
As if it had always been there, like a field
Full of silence, that is not beginning or ending.
It is so simple. You just hadn't looked.
And then you did, and couldn't look away.

Le Départ

You've been leaving for years and now no one's surprised
When you knock to come in from the weather.
The crew is past embarrassment:
They can live with their nautical names, and with yours.
So sit, take down your glass, and talk
Of all that is not you, that keeps you here
Among the sentimental stevedores
In the drinking clubs in the dank afternoons
Of your twenty-ninth year. There may be news.

Indeed. Somebody drowned last night, walked sideways
Off a Polish fishmeal hulk. A rabid Paraguayan bear
Was seen among the kindly hookers eating fruit.
A hand-carved coelacanth was found
When the cells were dug out to lay drains . . .

How can you not be struck by these arrivals?
The perfect boat is sailing Tuesday week.
It's heading southwards, way beyond the ice –
Starsailing seems quite plausible by night.
Until then there is querulous Ninepin
(The loss of his ticket for thieving)
And Madeleine's never-secret grief
(Be kind, and ask politely what)
And someone selling crocodiles
And hash from the sump of a jungle . . .
Now even the Juvaro have secret accounts –
Sell them your Service Forty-Five
And get a tape-recorder back . . .
The Amazon's an answering service:
No one's ever really lost. A month ago
Rocheteau, stuck for credit, offered up

The pelvic bones of Mungo Park
In exchange for a fifth of Jim Beam . . .
We always thought that Scot was lying about Africa.

It is easily night: soft boom of lighter-boats
Beyond the fogwall, swung on inauthentic tides
That left you here, that left you here
As the lovesongs go over the warehouse
Among patrolling cats and a lost ARP
With his bucket of sand and his halberd.

You are doped on the stairs on the way to the moon
With Yvonne, who has aged but not quite,
Who knows the words to every song
And places one flattering palm on your spine
Till you move, who keeps a special bottle
For you (but half gone, half gone) by the bed,
A black fire of sugar that says all there is
About travelling. You're halfway there.

And all shall sing the awful morning
Reminds them of themselves,
Then sleep in early restaurants,
Boastful of such daft endurance,
And then inspect the shipping lists
Until the time is right.

'You talk in your sleep,' says Yvonne.
'So I woke you. All this travelling –
You leave the girls for what?
Are we not always, always travelling?
Let's drink to that, and one before you go.'

The Police

No one believes them. Their windows get broken.
It rains in their yards and their kids
Dress in black and are sullen and pasty.
Their wives would like going to hangings:
They knit and they think about crime.

The police, they have allotments, too:
Like us they don't get paid.
But their beans are like stone
And their lettuce like kelp
And black men come on moonless nights
To burn the greenhouse down,
And their windows are broken
So they don't eat tomatoes.
The police, when they pot their begonias,
Press down with both thumbs, like that,
And a fly can be killed with one blow.

They are not jealous, the police.
When they stare at your allotment
They're sure there's a body below.
But if you say, 'Yes, he's a Roman,'
They ask you, 'And how do you know?'
We are all called *Sunshine*,
Or else we are liars, or both.
We would be better off without ourselves,
Or cordoned off, at least.
The world is guilty of itself,
Except the police, that is.

The police are not immortal, though they try.
They are buried with honours and bicycle clips.
But black men come from the allotments
And chop their gravestones down.
Then lots of queers with foreign names
Dig them up and make films of their bones.

The Beat Goes On

For Jerry Kidd and John Rowley

The radio's remembering
Piano-shifting brutalists
In suits of whorish pink, who vocalize
Bluenote-bayous of razz and grief; remembering
Mulatto chords and Mama Roux,
The currency and then the price
The stovepipe-hatted obeah man exacts
For stealing shellac masters
From the tombs of Creole Pharoahs
Still cool in their coke-filled sarcophagi
Under the boardwalks of Hell; remembering
The life we never lived
Again, a riding cymbal-shimmer
Stroked with a hickory Premier C
As the horns stand up in the key of real sex.
Encyclopaedias of air encode
The glamour of the singing poor.
We learn them like a second heart.
They gave the mirror all its moves:
Tonight it will not even laugh –
And for this I have drummed out the grease
From a lifetime of antimacassars,
Nagged by good taste and a future
That looks as high and lonesome now
As a busload of drunks and their delicate axes
Marooned in the snowy Sierras.
There's no cenotaph for those
Who try to cut the cost of touring,
Who go in derailments, in cropdusters' biplanes,
To Klansmen at crossroads,
Shot by their mistreated girls

Or drowned in concrete by the Mob,
And they cannot now honour their contract
To make us a language of passion and style.
But this evening the Sixties,
This evening the King,
So bored he even broadcasts hymns
To the wives of Nebraska and Kansas,
Who sweat at the prospect of leisure
And choke on their sociables, feeling Him move
In the air over wheatfields and highways.
The King keeps his class in the bathroom
With the whips and methadone.
He turns the Baptist Gospel off
And hears the princes practise down the hall.
They are harder and blacker and closer to jail
And the heartbreaking four forty-nine.
Tonight the trailer park gets drunk
Beneath a moon of impotence
As someone seminal awakes
At the wheel of a stolen Chevrolet,
To search the airwaves once again
For something that could make him dance,
With whisky freezing on his shirt
And a writ for his skin in his pocket.

The Lamp

Slowly, these evenings, it warms to its business,
Adding its ivory miniature wattage
To headaches unbidden or begged for;
To love doing overtime, vicious or civil.
A simple but brilliant composure
Of levers and springs, with a bulb and a flex,
It should be an eye but is not, and should know
But does not, and should feel but cannot.
It squats at my shoulder and silently stares,
Giving nothing away of the dreams it can't have.
These dreams concern high cold
And long views from a clinic to Europe
Set out beneath its haze of sun
And politics. No loneliness, no cry,
Can climb to the terrace where money is dying,
In rarefied purple, with desperate good humour.
The lamp is in place by the notes on the desk
In the room that is kept at the dry heat of health
And has four walls of medical journals.
Nobody lives here and no one is missing.
Strange if when some modernist made this
He failed to see its perfect sex. Plug in, turn on
And leave alone: blank ecstasy
Unbounded by the mortal physics.
An anglepoise lamp done in white.
If you were to ask me that now I should act
In reasonable faith to find a name
For what it does, then I would have to say,
You asking me, you being you, and reason being
What it is, and the lamp being here,
A prosthetic of dark in the room,
It sheds light, I suppose. *It depends what you mean.*

The Amateur God

Like sluggish electrons
The first gnats of April
Are cruising the visual field.
The kingfisher's moulting its plaster of Paris.
The cherub is moulting his head.
The goldfish stare upwards from cushions of weed,
Rehearsing blasé vowels at the sun.
The Peace Rose,
Pruned to a barbed-wire paradox,
Stands with its label, as if on a platform
Awaiting the slow train of summer.
The gardener beats a new path out of cinder.
The brazier rolls its crimson eyes
Like Argus. There's nothing but detail
And leisure to name it, with one hand
To cool in the pond, and the other
Rubbing moss into my jeans
Wholeheartedly at thirty as at three.
The afternoon is permanent.
My father, my uncle, in suits of pale ash,
Are still sinking the black in the shade.
The voices of their politics
Are softer than the fountain's voice.
The afternoon is permanent.
The amateur god of this garden is me.

In a Military Archive

The mirror on this corridor
Detains them in its waiting-room.
Sporadically the backward clock
Remembers its authentic boom
And flings the dead men to their knees.
They rise. They smoke. They watch their hands.
They mend the furniture and read.
The King's Own —shire Ampersands,
Preserved as footnotes in the texts
Of Hockley, Blunden, Hart et al.,
At ease in the grave-geographies
Of Arras, Albert and Thiepval.
Now literature is sent, as once
Were razor-blades and letters,
That the dead may study suffering
In the language of their betters.

Song of the South

We change our cars and eat our meat.
There are no negroes on our street.
Our sons are sailing with the fleet.
We keep our mania discreet.

We take our secretaries on trips.
We have a taste for furs and whips.
We look to Panama for ships.
It hurts us when the market slips.

We place our cash in krugerrands.
We rule the waves, so say the bands
At Brighton, where we own the sands.
You won't find blood upon our hands.

Conservative in politics,
We have no time for lefty pricks
Who sympathize with wogs and spicks.
We print the kind of shit that sticks.

We even bought a moralist.
We fund his comic, keep him pissed.
Just now we need him to exist,
The sweaty little onanist.

It is of property we dream.
We like to think we are a team.
We think that poverty's a scream.
We're still more vicious than we seem.

And speaking of the next world war,
The bang we've all been waiting for,
We will survive: We are the law
That shuts and locks the shelter door.

London Road

As I walked out on London Road
Towards the close of day,
I grew confused, and it appeared
I must have lost my way,

For when I stopped and looked around
The hills of Housman's blue
Had ceased to be a colour
And become a point of view.

It matched the spanking outfits
Of the cops who blocked the road.
The only things they seemed to lack
Were bucketfuls of woad.

One said, 'Now son, what business
Takes you out beyond the pale?
Are you quite sure you're what you seem,
A blue Caucasian male?

'You wouldn't be a picket
Or a dike from CND?
We've orders from her Majesty
To round them up, you see.'

'I'm going down the pub,' I said,
'Like every Friday night.
If it's OK with you, I'd like
To exercise that right.'

Apparently this angered him:
He took me by the balls.
His breath was acrid in my face,
Like bullet-holes in walls.

'We're here tonight rehearsing
For insurgencies ahead,
And if you breathe a bloody word
We'll beat you nine parts dead.

'We'll ask the questions afterwards
And charge you for the mess.
There'll also be a list of crimes –
You'll find that you confess.

'There'll be no point in asking
For the date of your release:
These days we throw away the key
When folks disturb the police.

'Take our advice: get off the street.
Stay in and watch TV.
Unless the law is absolute
The people can't be free.'

I turned and passed a barrier
In fear of an attack.
It isn't safe on London Road
And I'm not going back,

For in that land of lost content
Where facts are redefined
I've seen the enemy within,
The ones I left behind,

And as I walked I heard a song
Stage-whispered on the air,
Subversive in its sentiment,
The sound of no one there:

You poets of the little songs
Devoted to the muse –
You shouldn't be surprised, my lads,
To find you sing the blues.

The Mechanical Toy Museum

In the mechanical toy museum
At the end of Brighton's Palace Pier
Ten new pence will buy five old,
For history suffers inflation as well

And Jean Boudin might not believe
How big the smudged brown coins appear,
Designed to fit a pauper's eyes
Or the Jolly Nigger's thrifty tongue.

But no one is short of a penny in here
And that crimson-lipped, liquorice
Cast-iron slave is not one of the relics
Preserved in this tomb of Amusements.

Take care. These are delicate engines.
The pin-table predates the tilt,
Two threadbare teams stand riveted
In goalless extra time and the girls

In the peepshow must never be still
Or their bones will step out of their skins.
It keeps you fingering your change,
This taste for proofs of entropy.

Best of all, watch the beheading.
'Madame Guillotine est morte,'
A visitor carefully tells his son,
Who is keen to observe the procedure again.

But when the Bastille springs open,
Why, every time, does it seem that the corpse
Will pluck the straws from his spouting neck,
Take up his peruked head and walk

With an absolute confidence back
Down the mad-mirrored ormolu halls
Of the *ancien régime*, as if we had
Never existed, still less eaten cake?

Cousin Coat

You are my secret coat. You're never dry.
You wear the weight and stink of black canals.
Malodorous companion, we know why
It's taken me so long to see we're pals,
To learn why my acquaintance never sniff
Or send me notes to say I stink of stiff.

But you don't talk, historical bespoke.
You must be worn, be intimate as skin,
And though I never lived what you invoke,
At birth I was already buttoned in.
Your clammy itch became my atmosphere,
An air made half of anger, half of fear.

And what you are is what I tried to shed
In libraries with Donne and Henry James.
You're here to bear a message from the dead
Whose history's dishonoured with their names.
You mean the North, the poor, and troopers sent
To shoot down those who showed their discontent.

No comfort there for comfy meliorists
Grown weepy over Jarrow photographs.
No comfort when the poor the state enlists
Parade before their fathers' cenotaphs.
No comfort when the strikers all go back
To see which twenty thousand get the sack.

Be with me when they cauterize the facts.
Be with me to the bottom of the page,
Insisting on what history exacts.
Be memory, be conscience, will and rage,
And keep me cold and honest, cousin coat,
So if I lie, I'll know you're at my throat.

66

Kingdom of Kiev, Rios das Muertes

All afternoon, the streets are deaf with snow,
Its dripping dud piano muted,
The fire in the garden silently burning,
The visitors visiting others. Midwinter.
Words grow from each other to conquer the board
With childhood's careful mania.
The Kingdom of Kiev is colder than Hell
And Los Rios das Muertes are many –
Lies concerning geography,
The inexhaustible resource
From the era of General Knowledge,
Where Tupper and Wilson still circle the track
And an amateur Norwegian goalie
Whose name I'm afraid I've forgotten
Has kept a clean sheet for three years.
Consider the baking of salmon
In riverbank mud, and the means of ensuring
That wells dug in marshland run clear,
The feathers, the lead, how high the moon
And what precisely Grant had drunk
At Appomattox – useful stuff,
Assuming six times six will still
Fend off the nuns and chewing-gum
Enfolds the heart, and the air-bubble
Trapped in the co-pilot's molar explodes
At twenty thousand over Skaggarak . . .
If the Kingdom of Kiev is colder than Hell
Take furs to exchange and be careful
To sip the right side of the fiery bowl,
Not forgetting the boxes of Dickens.
If Los Rios das Muertes are many,

Choose one and remember your journal:
Observe how it breaks into leaf.
Slip a hand in the wet-velvet blackness
By night, in the squamous dun khaki by day.
Honour your dad on his moped,
Come home bearing gifts from the blizzard –
In Muscovy, *The Fawcett Expedition*,
Marrying tundra and tropic
As suitable places for anyone versed
In the pointless collection of facts.
The telephone won't ring, but if it does
I'll know until I pick it up
That the atlas has finally called.

The Head Man

For Margoulis Grolsz

You say you've been back for a look.
You're struck by the impressive podium,
The throne in which the Head Man sat
And ground his teeth with gout,
Dispensing justice and the lash
To the 'conference of funeral directors'
Who listened in pustular torpor
From the Main Hall's fog of breakfast farts
To the news that we could not speak English
Or read it, and ought to avoid it,
And worst of all ate in the street
Without caps on. Ah yes,
I remember it well, being frightened and wrong
On a permanent basis, secure
In the knowledge you'd never be short of a row,
And the lesson remains,
In this world of strong women
Who put me in mind of that pantomime demon
Revolving the dice in his head to decide
If today was for charm or for excoriation.
I stuck to my books, but my verses were proof
That the Russians had sent me
To fire the Hall, rape Edna the typist,
Abstract the school fund and be famous
And not know the value of money.
In fact all I stole was a copy
Of *Culture and Anarchy*. Touchstone, indeed:
It retains its original boredom,
Safe and stale in custard covers.
I read it last night when you'd rung,

Fell asleep and then dreamed of the journey
We'd talked our way out of for years –
By Araguaya, Negro and Las Muertes
To the utmost Amazonas, by canoe,
Our only plan: escape the map!
In the feverish heaven of jiggers,
Long after the final dry sock and the whisky,
Sick of mandioca, sick of fish,
Where the river runs into the sky and the trees
Form an endless and foetid arcade
With the promise of nothing beyond it – lost,
With the whole undertaking distinctly
Like something in Conrad gone wrong,
We arrived in the clearing, in which stood the hut
With its trellis of head-sporting poles.
When we ventured inside he was there,
Drinking port from a skull, reading Arnold
And saying, 'Late again. Explain yourselves.'

Geography

For Gerry

Tonight the blue that's flowing in
Beneath the window gloves my hands
With coolness, as indifferent as a nurse.
The ridge of forest wears grey smoke
Against grey pink, then deeper blue
Discloses what I cannot see,
The channel's distant bays, their sands
Drawn into shape by bows of surf,
Then further capes and promontories,
Sea-pines and isthmuses and island stepping
Out from island, all
Remoter than a name can reach.
Out there is home, a hammered strand
By some unvisitable sea,
Beyond all empire and all sense,
Enduring minus gender, case and tense,
A landfall, past imagining and free.

Before

Make over the alleys and gardens to birdsong,
The hour of not-for-an-hour. Lie still.
Leave the socks you forgot on the clothesline.
Leave slugs to make free with the pansies.
The jets will give Gatwick a miss
And from here you could feel the springs
Wake by the doorstep and under the precinct
Where now there is nobody frozenly waiting.
This is free time, in the sense that a handbill
Goes cartwheeling over the crossroads
Past stoplights rehearsing in private
And has neither witness nor outcome.
This is before the first bus has been late
Or the knickers sought under the bed
Or the first cigarette undertaken,
Before the first flush and cross word.
Viaducts, tunnels and motorways: still.
The mines and the Japanese sunrise: still.
The high bridges lean out in the wind
On the curve of their pinkening lights,
And the coast is inert as a model.
The wavebands are empty, the mail unimagined
And bacon still wrapped in the freezer
Like evidence aimed to intrigue our successors.
The island is dreamless, its slack-jawed insomniacs
Stunned by the final long shot of the movie,
Its murderers innocent, elsewhere.
The policemen have slipped from their helmets
And money forgets how to count.
In the bowels of Wapping the telephones
Shamelessly rest in their cradles.

The bomb in the conference centre's
A harmless confection of elements
Strapped to a duct like an art installation.
The Première sleeps in her fashion,
Her Majesty, all the princesses, tucked up
With the Bishops, the glueys, the DHSS,
In the People's Republic of Zeds.
And you sleep at my shoulder, the cat at your feet,
And deserve to be spared the irruption
Of if, but and ought, which is why
I declare this an hour of general safety
When even the personal monster –
Example, the Kraken – is dead to the world
Like the deaf submarines with their crewmen
Spark out at their fathomless consoles.
No one has died. There need be no regret,
For we do not exist, and I promise
I shall not wake anyone yet.

In the Other Bar

Forever a winter too old,
With her manners not quite of the moment,
She's wearing it well, the bad sister of London.

For all that the young are pronouncing
On art and safe sex, they will never belong
Where the numberless theatres are dark,

Where the numberless writers have stalled
At the peak of a small reputation
Caressed in damp stacks of *Horizon*,

Which mingles with *Lilliput*, not to deny
The Fitzrovian marriage of letters and smut.
Here the long honeymoon

Waged from Black Rock to the borders of Hove
Will go on so long as a thimble of gin
Can be traced between now and five thirty,

Ensuring the casual entrance of someone
Surprised to be here at this ticklish hour.
Beneath the slow wink of the optic there follows

The search for the chequebook, the novel
To rest on the bar while she smokes
And instructs us that boredom requires

A talent before which the proper responses
Are envy, humility, unbidden refills
And goes-without-saying acceptance

That she makes her entrance once only.
Her friends are the footnotes of footnotes,
Her lovers gone down in the Med

Or the annals of Gordon's, and she
Who has posed and factotumed forever
Could always have been what she chose,

But did not, d'you see, as it happens.
It's almost like love, to be met by a vanity
Nothing corrupts, which is always at home

And has nothing in mind but itself,
The whole lifetime of elegant, objectless
Fucking and fighting, despair as a style

In the district of post-dated cheques
And not-quite prostitution,
Blank beyond judgement and not to be missed.

And when you come back from a pee
She has left you a stool and an ashtray.
Then later when walking through streets

Which can still catch the sun
There is someone who might be an actress
Whose name you can almost remember,

Glimpsed high on a balcony, resting
And staring straight through you
And keeping her looks in this light.

Propaganda

After the whole abandoned stretch,
The bricked-up arches, flooded birchwoods,
The miniature oxbows and dubious schools,
After the B-roads that curved out of sight
Beneath bridges to similar views,
All the scenery hauled away backwards
While this train was heading elsewhere,
After the threat to our faith in the railways,
It seems that at last we have come to the place
That described us before we were thought of.
We stand on its sweltering, porterless platform
And wait in the time-honoured manner.
The stalled afternoon's like a story
Once left on a train with a chapter to go,
Smelling of oil, of dust and old sunlight.
Here are the canopy, flowertubs, posters for war
And the bum-frying torpor of benches.
Here are the smoke in the throat of the tunnel,
The footbridge a guess in the glare, and the clank
As the points irreversibly switch, and here
Is the perfect assurance that somewhere
Close by it is quietly happening.

It's here that Germany in person calls
By parachute, at first confused to death
By Brough and Slough, by classroom spinsters
Jumping on the hand-grenades. Their dull reports
Alert the author sleeping at his desk,
The curate and the mower in the fields.
A bucket fills and overflows, abandoned
To blacken the stones of a whitewashed yard.
In the brown upper rooms there are women

Attending to letters. We are not permitted
To stand at their shoulders and may not
Determine the date, but the subject
Is things going on as they must, the summer
Still adding fresh months to itself, and the way
You'd never guess by simply looking round.

How easy to know where we stand, within sight
Of the back-to-front fingerpost, certain
That commandeered railings still rust
In the sidings, that somewhere up there
In the ferns is what looks like a gate
But is really a lock on the gelid
Forgotten canal, that its waters retain
All their monochrome heat and exist
For the drenching of constables.
O Mr Porter, the convicts are coming,
Ineptly, their suits full of arrows,
Over the dismal, bunkered levels,
Still sawing their irons and shouting.

It's midnight. On schedule, the ghost train
Is failing the bend by the claypits,
And stiff with old service revolvers,
Unsleeping on hard wooden chairs –
The price of this unnecessary trip –
We stare at the waiting-room fireplace and know
That the corpse in its bundle of coats
Will awake and the door be flung open
When Hammerpond enters, no longer a tramp,
To deliver the long explanation
Whose end we will miss when the radio coughs
And announces that all roads are flooded,
The sovereign's in Canada, Hitler in Brighton,
And no one will leave here tonight.

Boundary Beach

Invalids, perverts, and chambermaids born to be duped,
And those characters never awarded a name
Who must pass just before and just after the moment
And never be wiser: they have been here.

And the bad men themselves, stepping on to the grass
With a hum of the sexual magnet, were here.
The bad women whom cash and contempt had enraged
Were seen waiting, the sisters of Ruth, to be hanged

All along the blue border of Sussex and England
Where everything stops, even money, on Boundary Beach.
They arrived in their fugitive tenses, like art.
One would ladder a stocking, another count change

In the torment of not-quite-enough, and the third be on hand
With a wallet to match the occasion, a car
And the promise of waking up changed. They were English
And liked a good murder, the thrill of comeuppance

Achieved in the shelter behind the hotel. The detectives
Were born to the trade. Their exhaustion and fury
Would fill the slow shoes of the law, put its questions
From Volks to the fringes of Shoreham and go

Through the head-scratching, half-sipping migraine,
The grey, overheated minuteness that led
To the tawdry perception – a ticket, a stain – and then on
To a room by the A23 and the motive. Imagine them

Coming downstairs with the knowledge,
The windowless corridors left with their keyholes
And Do Not Disturbs, their adulteries, there at the death
While a constable sat in the kitchen, his collar undone,

As he wiped his moustache free of mustard
And offered his view to a maid and the boots
Who would read the same evening a fuller report
And glance out at the darkness before turning in,

In a hundred hotels that claim views of the sea,
Where the sleepless are counting the waves,
All along the blue border of Sussex and England,
Where everything stops, even money, on Boundary Beach.

The Brighton Goodbye

This is the place we imagine we live,
Where the land slowly stops,
Among streets where the sea is implied
In white walls and expectant top windows
Left open for signals offshore.
The air is as bright as the harbour at noon
In the heat that can turn even cops into punters
And which we inhabit like natives of summer,
As if we had known it must come.
Now everyone seems to be leaving:
The bar-room will empty tonight
And be shuttered tomorrow,
A capsule of posters and still-sticky tables,
Its music absorbed into smoke.
The girl in the shop buying fruit
Has her mind on a schedule,
Her brown skin important with travel.
The old have prepared for a lifetime,
And now as they sit on their doorsteps
And wait to be told or collected
They cancel the hours with freesheets
Whose Gilbert and Sullivans, dogtracks
And fifteen quid bargains are clues
To a culture they've never known
Time or the passion to learn.
It is suddenly late. The afternoon yawns
And continues. A lean-to of shade
In a sunken backyard is the colour
Of Indian ink at the moment
The ferry swings out of the bay,
When the sea has no need to be local
And shows you the colour it keeps for itself,
Which you look at with terror and love.

Betweentimes

There is an hour waiting in between.
In ruined districts, blue light waits.
Wrecking-yards and bar-rooms wait.
You can study the dust in the windows
Of incomprehensible premises, guess
At the null carborundum, clamped to its bench,
At all the further streets these streets conceal –

Their distant interiors, pillars of air
Under skylights where somebody stood
For a smoke, at the pinups entombed
In the necropolis of lockers, at calendars,
Invoices, indents of chair-legs in floorboards,
At tab-ends in cold-stores, and voices you know
Are not talking tonight after work.

No clockface admits it, the in-between hour.
Over the road an old barmaid of thirty
Rehearses a spin on high white heels
And supplies, unrequested, a pint
To the old man re-reading the paper.
You'd think they had built this around him,
Brick and varnish, optics, disappointment.

This is how waiting turns into a life,
In the hour it seems would explain
If the mind could forget what it thinks
About failure and history and money, and watch
How aesthetics takes leave of its senses,
In love with the facts of the matter,
The blue light and derelict happiness.

HMS Glasshouse

At this hour the park offers only
A steam-heated acre of glass,
A sign in fresh hardboard, and somewhere
To wait while appearing to act.

We step inside its vaulted heat,
Its bleared below-decks light. We taste
Its air of rot and counter-rot, attend
Its vegetable politics, and watch

As plants with webbed and shellacked hands
Swarm up the stanchions, offering
The universal shrug of making do,
Like the teenagers painting the catwalks,

Who might once have painted the hulls
Of the frigates and merchantmen sent
To secure the Malvinas for mutton.
Their status as national assets has lapsed

And the registers cancel their names:
They are guilty again, as am I, as are you,
As the glasshouse sweats on
Like the *Unterseeboot* of the state

With its periscope down, its orders sealed,
Its routine a deliberate torpor.
We wake in the very same place
With the curious notion that fish

Have been crowding the glass to peer in
At the items preserved for the voyage –
Cast-iron and Pilkingtons' finest,
Odd volumes of Oakeshott and Scruton

To kill off the time, in an atmosphere
Soon to be poison. Let's make our inspection
On tiptoe, and listen for cracks
In case one of us throws the first stone.

Ballad of the Lit and Phil

When I went in that afternoon
With work that must be done
I should have left the books at home
And fetched a scatter-gun.

For all that things seemed quiet
In the varnished vestibule
The maze of galleries beyond
Was given to misrule,

And the enemies of silence
Were waiting in the stacks
And at a given signal
Commenced with their attacks:

To start with, just the graveyard cough,
The snigger and the snerk,
Then someone bawling, *Mustn't chat —
I've come in here to work*,

But somehow taking ages
To get the one thing said,
And hovering, and fingering
The Listener instead.

Thus the hours screamed away,
Distracted into dust,
But there were deadlines to be met —
I worked because I must.

I bowed my head and thumbed my ears
And damned if I'd give up.
One broke a chair. Another dropped
His top set in my cup,

And then the tea-lady came singing
And a-banging of her tray,
So clearly they could keep this up
The livelong bloody day.

Some others murdered violins
Somewhere beneath my feet
And blokes came in with spades and dug
The place up like a street.

But still I smiled and held my peace
And laboured down the page,
Until at last a silence fell
Like acid-drops of rage

Through which there came to sit with me
A leading local bore.
He told me how much parquet
Went to lay the library floor,

And how the old librarians
Would mix the morning's ink
And how much sugar Marat took
In what he liked to drink . . .

This last (alas) was interesting
And took me off my guard,
And glimpsing opportunity
He smiled and came in hard.

Please understand, this is a place
For people who pretend.
If someone tries to work in here
It drives us round the bend.

You think this is a library?
It's the temple of a sect
Whose article of faith
Is simple: Only disconnect.

We view ourselves as guardians
Of ignorance and sloth,
And no one stays a member here
Unless he swears to both.

Everywhere and always, friend,
Since language first was stored —
The mass of membership has been
A vast illiterate fraud.

Bodley, Austin, Pierpont Morgan,
Big UL and old BM —
Oh do you seriously think
That anybody reads in them?

And I dreamed a dream of libraries
Exactly as he said,
Repositories of indolence
Where nothing's ever read,

From Adelaide to Antioch,
From Zanzibar to Nome,
A vast deliberate vacancy,
An overarching dome.

The vision was the weariness
Ecclesiastes meant,
And suddenly I understood
The reason I'd been sent,

And why my hopes of wisdom
Were mere errors in the text.
O reader, can you understand
The thing that I did next?

Tenderly I took his head
And bashed it on the floor.
The next I knew, librarians
Were showing me the door.

They threw me out into the street
Where I am lying now.
They made me give my ticket back.
They said I made a row.

And now I'm banned from every
Bloody branch in town,
But I shall visit them by night
And burn the bastards down.

Oh weep for Alexandria,
That library-lacuna,
But left to me it would have turned
To ash a good deal sooner.

Working on the Railway

You are trying to work but you sit
With the wrong book entirely: *Lost Railways of England*,
Whose dust of the forties, the fifties,
Is making you sneeze. When you just have a look
At the picture of steam as it swallows the bridge
At Botanic, you're going. Then Stepney, Stoneferry
And Wilmington. Flatlands. The vanished resorts
Where the girls run down into the water
Like spies with a half-hour free,
Then back to the baker's, the nightschool,
The sombre saloon of the Station Hotel.
Past the window the *Montague Finnegan*
Pulls away north, and the soldiers are crowding
The corridors, wishing that girls were laid on
To be waving farewell, like the future,
A bed you need never get out of.
From there you could grasp it, the railway,
The sea creaming in at the piers,
And just round the corner the carriages stand
In the first of the heat, with their headachy air
Full of dustmotes, their pictures of elsewhere:
An hour of silence that seems to be England,
The life it was offered once only,
Its trivial, infinite distances –
Promises, promises. Write it all down.

Serious

Let us be serious now, says the teacher,
Inserting a pause in the hot afternoon
As she steeples her fingers and waits.

It's hard not to look at the snow
That prolongs the blue end of the day,
Not to think of it gathered

In alleys and gardens across the flat town
For a footprint, but this is Miss Garvin
And those are her fingers,

And though her long nails are a vanity
None of the sisters approves,
She speaks as they speak, for a power

That means us to answer the serious question
We have not been asked, that we cannot imagine
Or fail to be wrong in attempting:

Therefore we are serious now, as we wonder
Who might be the shameful example
To prove the unspecified point.

It may lie in the fork of a crocus
Or bury a jamjar left out on the step,
Or fall in its passion for detail

On two unburnt coals in the grate,
But the snow cannot help or survive
In the heat of the serious moment,

The void of all content
Where something, as ever, is wrong.
Across the yard the boilers roar.

Good children, we long to be serious well,
To multiply the word on slates,
To raise our voices in its name

And wear its ash with modesty.
We slip our hands behind the pipes
And turn them into gloves of pain.

A Corridor

For Henry Katz

The shoulder-high tiles in municipal green,
The brown walls, the bare lavatorial floor
Which is always about to be damp,
The heavy swing doors we shall not
Be exploring today; the long view
We are taking this late afternoon –
Whose end is obscure
With November indoors, it would seem –
In the fifties, when we were much smaller
And quickly impressed by the minor displays
Of the State which would aim us
From cradle to grave, you remember:
All this we inherit, a corridor
Built by the Irish for God and the Queen.

We trap our germs in handkerchiefs.
We do not spit when on the bus.
Out where the city once turned into fields
Are prefabs growing permanent:
To each its patch of grass, from each a vote.
And here where the corridor turns in a fury of echoes
My father is leaving the party for nowhere,
The intimate cell where the struggle is waged
Over doughnuts in Lyons, the afternoons hung
With sheets of Players, the talk of betrayal.
It's what lies before us when we are too old
To be sure – which was never his problem.
The problems he had were the world
And his terrible spelling, I'm told.
They have rolled up the speeches, the grass from the park
After Mayday and stored them in here.

Behind the baize door a committee
Is handing the scholarships out –
A regime of deaf butchers and bandit accountants
Rewarded for lifetimes of ignorance,
Waiting to get our names wrong.
In the clinic a sinister lady
Will study my feet and insist
I can reach the trapeze.
My grandfather wheels a dead man
To the morgue for a pittance
And votes the wrong way as a duty
To something the next war was meant to disprove.
We vanish to Mafeking, Simla,
The moth-eaten middle of Ireland
Where Marx is a nightmare
That God isn't having
And people like us are a gleam of prolepsis
In somebody's eye – the well-meaning
Impotent heirs to the corridor,
Pacing it out past the dinner-money's chink,
Cries from the dentist and telephones nobody answers,
Incompetent dreaming, corrupt and forgetful,
The cellars of pamphlets for futures
That nobody lived. This is ours. Keep walking.

After Laforgue

In memory of Martin Bell

I have put a blockade on high-mindedness.
All night, through dawn and dead mid-morning,
Rain is playing rimshots on a bucket in the yard.
The weatherman tells me that winter comes on
As if he'd invented it. Fuck him.

Fuck sunshine and airports and pleasure.
Wind is deadheading the lilacs inland.
You know what this means. I could sing.
The weekend sailors deal the cards and swear.
The Channel is closed. This is good.

In the sopping, padlocked, broad-leaved shade of money
Desperate lunches are cooking
In time for the afternoon furies and sudden
Divorces of debt from the means of production.
Good also. These counties are closed.

Myself, I imagine the north in its drizzle,
Its vanished smoke, exploded chimneys: home
In bad weather to hills of long hospitals, home
To the regional problems of number, home
To sectarian strife in the precincts of Sheffield and Hartlepool,

Home from a world of late-liberal distraction
To rain and tenfoots clogged with leaves,
To the life's work of boredom and waiting,
The bus-station's just-closing teabar,
The icy, unpromising platforms of regional termini,

Home to dead docks and the vandalized showhouse.
Home for Mischief Night and Hallowe'en, their little tales,
When the benches (the sodden repose of old bastards in dog-
    smelling overcoats)
Vanish, when council employees dragged from the pub
Will be dragging the lake in the park,

Watching their footprints fill up
And hating those whose bastard lives
Are bastard lived indoors. Home,
As Sunday extends towards winter, a shivery kiss
In a doorway, *Songs of Praise*, last orders. Home.

Rain, with an angel's patience, remind me.
This is not the world of Miss Selfridge and Sock Shop,
Disposable income and lycra, illiterate hearsay
And just-scraping-in-after-Clearing to Business in Farnham.
This world is not Eastbourne. It has no opinions.

In this world it rains and the winter
Is always arriving – rebirth of TB
And *The Sporting Green* sunk to the drainbed.
Here is the stuff that gets left in the gaps
Between houses – ambitious settees in black frogskin

And minibars missing their castors, the catalogues
Turning to mush, the unnameable objects
That used to be something with knobs on,
And now they live here, by the siding, the fishhouse,
The building whose function is no longer known.

It is Londesborough Street with the roof gone –
That smell as the wallpaper goes, as it rains
On the landing, on pot dogs and photos
And ancient assumptions of upright servility.
Nothing is dry. The pillow-tick shivers

And water comes up through the scullery tiles
And as steam from the grate. There are funerals
Backed up the street for a mile
As the gravediggers wrestle with pumps and the vicar
Attempts to hang on to his accent.

Rain, with an angel's patience, teach me
The lesson of where I came in once again,
With icy vestibules and rubber pillows,
The dick-nurse, the wet-smelling ash in the yard
And the bleary top deck like a chest-ward.

Teach me the weather will always be worsening,
With the arctic fleet behind it –
The subject of talk in the shop, at the corner,
Or thought of when stepping out into the yard
To the sirens of factories and pilot-boats,

There like a promise, the minute at nightfall
When rain turns to snow and is winter.

Somebody Else

In fact you are secretly somebody else.
You live here on the city's edge
Among back lanes and stable-blocks
From which you glimpse the allegations
Of the gardening bourgeoisie that all is well.
And who's to argue? Lilac's beaten to the punch
By cherry blossom and the spire disappears
Among the leaves. Merely to think of
The ground-cover detail this outline implies,
The seeds and saplings and their names,
The little wayside trestles where they're bought,
The just-so cafés, the innumerable
And unnumbered high-hedged roads
For coming home down sleepily,
For instance – that would blind you
With a migraine, were one possible
In this redemptive climate. Sit.

It is somewhere you thought you had seen
From a train. You were not coming here.
It is something you thought was a striking vignette
By an as-yet-uncredited hand. It is somewhere
In moments of weakness at Worcester Shrub Hill
Or in Redditch or Selby you wished
You could enter. You already had. This is it,
The good place, unencumbered by meaning.
For hours no one comes or goes:
The birds, the light, the knowledge
That this place is endlessly repeated –
Is the known world and the elsewheres too –
Will do the living for you. Were you moved
To halve a gravestone you might find
That *England, 2pm* was written through it.

Long before now you've imagined
A woman at work in an attic,
Applying the back of her elegant wrist
To a strand of loose hair. She was sorting
A life, in a shaft of pale dust
Where a slate had come loose, but now
She is quite frankly reading. Kneeling
By a doll's house full of Guardsmen
She's stunned by what she thought she thought.
In the kitchen three storeys below
Are an unopened newspaper next to the hob
And a cat coming in, going out,
Like a trouper, addressing its bowl
In the permanent meantime through which
You come walking so fluently
People would think you belong.
As to the man in her life,
If you lived at a different hour
You'd see him performing his vanishing act
On the bridge by the station.
The train doesn't come, only noises.
A stiff breeze unsettles the fireweed,
Leading the eye to the drop where the stream,
Which is almost as real as the Boat Race,
Goes quietly down to the bend where it vanishes too.
As to sex, you have gained the impression
That somehow it's meant to encourage the others
Who might overrate or not do it at all,
Either way missing the point, although no one
As far as you know has yet clarified that.
The tree-shadows washing the ceiling,
The damp patch in bed, and her manner,
Both brisk and erotic, of pausing
To put up her hair before dressing,
All these suggest you are here.

What, then, of scholarship?
In the 'history room' whose fake stained glass
Is viewed with that tolerant humour
(What isn't?) are somebody's books
In a version of English you half understand.
You search the catalogue
Of the Festival of Britain
Repeatedly for evidence of you
And think it must have been mislaid.
When will you learn? What could it mean,
Conspiracy, when everyone conspires
Against themselves and does not know it?

A Rarity

It's under the X where the viaducts met.
It was round the back and further down
And it isn't that street but a vanished
Identical elsewhere that waits
In a different night with a different accent
Beneath a blue sign reading TIXE.
Kelly's *Apocrypha* offers no entry
But don't let that stop you from wasting
The middling years in pursuit of a number
Whose title escapes you, a band you can't
Even remember or swear to have heard.
Polish your shoes, climb into bed
And breathe in the sweetness of nylon and Bass.
The girls are done up to the nines,
Like racoons with affective disorders,
Rehearsing three steps round their handbags
And speaking in smoke-rings, a code
Meaning *Fuck off and die* or *Be older*,
Knowing it's to you the management reserves
The right to do pre-emptive violence.
You almost believe in the night you went
In on a whim and came out on a stretcher
With VOX back-to-front on your forehead.
Rippling in its skin of sweat
The bar retires to infinity, bulb
After bulb swinging back to the stillness
Your dreaming's disrupted, the night
Before music and after, the night of un-music –
No horn-chart, no thin, underamplified Fender,
No workaday-beautiful backline, no voice
Being torn from the soles of the feet:

No such matrix, no such number.
Everything is afterwards, a dripping jacket
Hung across a mirror, drinks becoming syrup,
A van spitting teeth on its way to the knacker's.
The culture of almost is married, divorced
And has always been forty. Yet now you step in –
The wrong hole, the wrong wall, but at least
It's not there in the hours of business –
To run down a shuddering spiral that ends
In a foyer intriguingly minus a door.
Knee-deep in water and flyers, it smells
Like your big sister's hairspray, supposing
She'd used it or even existed.
Under the dandruff of whitewash and rust,
Behind traffic and ship-engines,
Wind in the stairwell, the pulse in your temple,
What you can hear will be nothing, the space
Made of wishing, the cousin of happiness,
Waiting to comfort the longing to know
There is something you still haven't got.
Why not pick up a leaflet? It mentions
The unnumbered white-label item
Unearthed by a rumour (one copy)
In Belgium. The price is an arm and a leg,
Your entire collection, your job and your marriage
And still you won't find it. It's perfect.

Essay on Snow

We have been here before, but not often,
With the blue snow lying on the shaded roofs
And the city beyond them
Lying open, miles of it, with no one there –

Untrodden parks and freezing underpasses,
The statuary anonymous, the cobbled chares
Like streams of blackened ice.
There is a bird somewhere. Its voice

Is like chipping an icicle,
Damping the note, then trying again.
We have lived in the wrong place forever,
But now we can see what we meant,

The blue snow-shade behind the house,
The abandoned allotment, the shed,
The rags of willowherb, the one-note
Samba of the bird inside the ice.

Reading Stevens in the Bath

It is Newcastle at evening. It is far
From the furnished banks of the coaly Tyne
But close beside the hidden and infernal banks

Of the unutterable Ouseburn. Howay. It cries
Its native cry, this poisoned soup of prawns.
Howay. The evil river sings. The mind,

In Forest Hall, the haunted disbelieving suburb
Like a field of snowmen, the mind in Forest Hall
Lays by its knitting and considers

Going to the Fusilier. Howay. But in the upper room,
The room upstairs, the upstairs room,
The blear of glass and heat wherein

Not much is visible, a large pink man
Is reading Stevens in the bath. Howay. It is bath-time,
The time of the bath, the green-watered, where the mind

Lies unencumbered by the body as by time.
It is the bath as absolute, admitting
No conditional of green, the bath in which the bather

Lies considering. And the mind takes out
Its lightness to inspect, and finding nothing there
Begins to sing, embodying, emboldening its note.

It is the singing body in the bath, the mind.
Bookless Fruiterers, tell me if you can
What he may find to sing about, that man

Half audible, and howling, as it were, the moon
That rests its gravity on weary Forest Hall,
That sends its tidal song by Tyne,

By Ouseburn, by the purifying plant
And ultimately here, to this balneum absolute,
Steam-punkah'd bath at the end of the mind, whose singer

Sings beyond the scope of tongues and sanity
Of neighbours, howling like a wolf among the snowmen
To the moon which does not listen:

Say it's only a paper moon,
Sailing over a cardboard sea,
But it wouldn't be make-believe

If you believed in me.
Howay. Howay. Howay!

Tony Harrison

Thomas Campey and the Copernican System

The other day all thirty shillings' worth
Of painfully collected waste was blown
Off the heavy handcart high above the earth,
And scattered paper whirled around the town.

The earth turns round to face the sun in March,
He said, resigned, *it's bound to cause a breeze.*
Familiar last straws. His back's strained arch
Questioned the stiff balance of his knees.

Thomas Campey, who, in each demolished home,
Cherished a Gibbon with a gilt-worked spine,
Spengler and Mommsen, and a huge, black tome
With Latin titles for his own decline:

Tabes dorsalis; veins like flex, like fused
And knotted flex, with a cart on the cobbled road,
He drags for life old clothing, used
Lectern bibles and cracked Copeland Spode,

Marie Corelli, Ouida and Hall Caine
And texts from Patience Strong in tortoise frames.
And every pound of this dead weight is pain
To Thomas Campey (Books) who often dreams

Of angels in white crinolines all dressed
To kill, of God as Queen Victoria who grabs
Him by the scruff and shoves his body pressed
Quite straight again under St Anne's slabs.

And round Victoria Regina the Most High
Swathed in luminous smokes like factories,
These angels serried in a dark, Leeds sky
Chanting *Angina —a, Angina Pectoris.*

Keen winter is the worst time for his back,
Squeezed lungs and damaged heart; just one
More sharp turn of the earth, those knees will crack
And he will turn his warped spine on the sun.

Leeds! Offer thanks to that Imperial Host,
Squat on its thrones of Ormus and of Ind,
For bringing Thomas from his world of dust
To dust, and leisure of the simplest kind.

The Pocket Wars of Peanuts Joe

'Poor old sport,
he got caught
right in the mangle.'

The *-nuts* bit really *-nis.* They didn't guess
Till after he was dead, then his sad name
Was bandied as a dirty backstreet Hess,
A masturbator they made bear the blame
For all daubed swastikas, all filthy scrawl
In Gents *and* Ladies, YANK GO HOME
Scratched with a chisel on the churchyard wall;
The vicar's bogey against wankers' doom.

We knew those adult rumours just weren't true.
We did it often but our minds stayed strong.
Our palms weren't cold and tacky and they never grew
Those tell-tale matted tangles like King Kong.
We knew that what was complicated joy
In coupled love, and for lonely men relief,
For Joe was fluted rifling, no kid's toy
He fired and loaded in his handkerchief.
Some said that it was shell-shock. They were wrong.
His only service was to sing *The Boers
Have Got My Daddy* and *The Veteran's Song*
And window-gazing in the Surplus Stores.
In allotment dugouts, nervous of attack,
Ambushing love-shadows in the park,
His wishes shrapnel, Joe's ack-ack *ejac-*
ulatio shot through the dark
Strewn, churned up trenches in his head.
Our comes were colourless but Joe's froze,
In wooshed cascadoes of ebullient blood-red,
Each flushed, bare woman to a glairy pose.

'VD Day' jellies, trestle tables, cheers
For Ruskis, Yanks and Desert Rats with guns
And braces dangling, drunk; heaped souvenirs:
Swastikas, Jap tin hats and Rising Suns.
The Victory bonfire settled as white ash.
The accordion stopped Tipperarying.
It was something solemn made Joe flash
His mitred bishop as they played *The King*.
Happy and Glorious . . . faded away. *Swine!*
The disabled veteran with the medals cried.
The ARP tobacconist rang 999.
The Desert Rats stood guard on either side.
Two coppers came, half-Nelsoned, frog-
marched poor Penis off to a cold clink.
He goosestepped backwards and crowds saw the cock
That could gush Hiroshimas start to shrink.

A sergeant found him gutted like a fish
On army issue blades, the gormless one,
No good for cannon fodder. His last wish
Bequeathed his gonads to the Pentagon.

Allotments

Choked, reverted *Dig for Victory* plots
Helped put more bastards into Waif Home cots
Than anywhere, but long before my teens
The Veterans got them for their bowling greens.
In Leeds it was never *Who* or *When* but *Where*.
The bridges of the slimy River Aire,
Where Jabez Tunnicliffe, for love of God,
Founded the *Band of Hope* in eighteen odd,
The cold canal that ran to Liverpool,
Made hot trickles in the knickers cool
As soon as flow. The graveyards of Leeds 2
Were hardly love-nests but they had to do –
Through clammy mackintosh and winter vest
And rumpled jumper for a touch of breast.
Stroked nylon crackled over groin and bum
Like granny's wireless stuck on Hilversum.
And after love we'd find some epitaph
Embossed backwards on your arse and laugh.
And young, we cuddled by the abattoir,
Faffing with fastenings, never getting far.
Through sooty shutters the odd glimpsed spark
From hooves on concrete stalls scratched at the dark
And glittered in green eyes. Cowclap smacked
Onto the pavings where the beasts were packed.
And offal furnaces with clouds of stench
Choked other couples off the lychgate bench.

The Pole who caught us at it once had smelt
Far worse at Auschwitz and at Buchenwald,
He said, and, pointing to the chimneys, *Meat!*
Zat is vere zey murder vat you eat.

And jogging beside us, *As Man devours*
Ze flesh of animals, so vorms devour ours.
It's like your anthem, Ilkla Moor Baht 'at.
Nearly midnight and that gabbling, foreign nut
Had stalled my coming, spoilt my appetite
For supper, and gave me a sleepless night
In which I rolled frustrated and I smelt
Lust on myself, then smoke, and then I felt
Street bonfires blazing for the end of war
V.E. and J. burn us like lights, but saw
Lush prairies for a tumble, wide corrals,
A Loiner's Elysium, and I cried
For the family still pent up in my balls,
For my corned beef sandwich, and for genocide.

The Nuptial Torches

'These human victims, chained and burning at the stake, were the
blazing torches which lighted the monarch to his nuptial couch.'
                              – J. L. Motley, *The Rise of the Dutch Republic*

Fish gnaw the Flushing capons, hauled from fleeced
Lutheran Holland, for tomorrow's feast.
The Netherlandish lengths, the Dutch heirlooms,
That might have graced my movements and my groom's
Fade on the fat sea's bellies where they hung
Like cover-sluts. Flesh, wet linen wrung
Bone dry in a washerwoman's raw, red,
Twisting hands, bed-clothes off a lovers' bed,
Falls off the chains. At Valladolid
It fell, flesh crumpled like a coverlid.

Young Carlos de Sessa stripped was good
For a girl to look at and he spat like wood
Green from the orchards for the cooking pots.
Flames ravelled up his flesh into dry knots
And he cried at the King: *How can you stare
On such agonies and not turn a hair?*
The King was cool: *My friend, I'd drag the logs
Out to the stake for my own son, let dogs
Get at his testes for his sins; auto-da-fés
Owe no paternity to evil ways.*
Cabrera leans against the throne, guffaws
And jots down to the Court's applause
Yet another of the King's *bons mots*.

O yellow piddle in fresh fallen snow –
Dogs on the Guadarramas . . . dogs. Their souls
Splut through their pores like porridge holes.
They wear their skins like cast-offs. Their skin grows
Puckered round the knees like rumpled hose.

Doctor Ponce de la Fuente, you,
Whose gaudy, straw-stuffed effigy in lieu
Of members hacked up in the prison, burns
Here now, one sacking arm drops off, one turns
A stubble finger and your skull still croons
Lascivious catches and indecent tunes;
And croaks: *Ashes to ashes, dust to dust.*
Pray God be with you in your lust.
And God immediately is, but such a one
Whose skin stinks like a herring in the sun,
Huge from confinement in a filthy gaol,
Crushing the hooping on my farthingale.

O Holy Mother, Holy Mother, Ho-
ly Mother Church, whose melodious, low
Labour-moans go through me as you bear
These pitch-stained children to the upper air,
Let them lie still tonight, no crowding smoke
Condensing back to men float in and poke
Their charcoaled fingers at our bed, and let
Me be his pleasure, though Philip sweat
At his rhythms and use those hateful tricks
They say he feels like after heretics.

O let the King be gentle and not loom
Like Torquemada in the torture room,
Those wiry Spanish hairs, these nuptial nights,
Crackling like lit tapers in his tights,
His seed like water spluttered off hot stone.
Maria, whose dark eyes very like my own
Shine on such consummations, Maria bless
My Philip just this once with gentleness.

The King's cool knuckles on my smoky hair!

Mare Mediterraneum, la mer, la mer
That almost got him in your gorge with sides
Of feastmeats, you must flush this sacred bride's
Uterus with scouring salt. O cure and cool
The scorching birthmarks of his branding-tool.

Sweat chills my small breasts and limp hands.

They curled like foetuses, *maman*, and cried.

His crusted tunics crumple as he stands:

Come, Isabella. God *is satisfied.*

The Bedbug

Comrade, with your finger on the playback switch,
Listen carefully to each love-moan,
And enter in the file which cry is real, and which
A mere performance for your microphone.

CURTAIN SONNETS

1. GUAVA LIBRE
For Jane Fonda, Leningrad, 1975

Pickled Gold Coast clitoridectomies?
Labia minora in formaldehyde?
A rose pink death mask of a screen cult kiss,
Marilyn's mouth or vulva mummified?

Lips cropped off a poet. That's more like.
That's almost the sort of poet I think I am.
The lips of Orpheus fished up by a dyke
singing 'Women of Cuba Libre and Vietnam!'

The taste, though, taste! Ah, that could only be

('Women! Women! O *abajo* men,
the thought of it's enough to make you come!')

the honeyed yoni of Eurydice

and I am Orpheus going down again –

Thanks for the guavas soaked in Cuban rum.

2. THE VIEWLESS WINGS
Monkwood, Grimley

The hungry generations' new decree
turns Worcester orchards into fields of sage.

Tipsy, courtesy cheap wine and EEC,
I hear, as unaware of ours as Keats's age,
the same blithe bird but its old magic fails
and my longing for you now is just as bad
at England's northern edge for nightingales
as those White Nights last year in Leningrad,
where, packed for my flight back, thick curtains drawn
but night too like full day to get much kip,
I wanted you to watch with me from bed
that seamless merger of half dusk and dawn,
AURORA, rosy-fingered kind, and battleship
whose sudden salvo turned the East half red.

3. SUMMER GARDEN

Winter false dawns woke me: *thud! thud! thud!*
Lorries loaded with chipped ice and not quite four!
Felt-swathed babushkas stooping to chip more –
Leningrad's vast pool of widowhood,
who also guard the Rembrandts and rank Gents,
who stand all day with stern unbending gaze
haloed with Tsars' crowns and Fabergés,
their menfolk melted down to monuments.

It's their eyes make me shy I've fallen for
a woman who they'd chorus at *nyet! nyet!*
and make me edgy walking here with you
between the statues VERITAS, HONOR
and PYSCHE, whom strong passion made forget
conditions of darkness and the gods' taboo.

4. THE PEOPLE'S PALACE

Shuffling in felt goloshes saves the floor
from the unexpected guests of history
who queue all day to see what once was for
the fruits of just one bonsai family tree.

IUSTITIA and POMONA in their crates.
Come winter and the art, all cordoned off,
's wired to a US import anti-theft device
and opened only for researching prof.
and *patineur* from Academe who skates
those ballrooms patterned like cracked Baikal ice
buffing the princely parquets for the few
who'll see them reproduced in some review.

Watch that elegant glissade as he yahoos
into the soundproof pile of overshoes.

5. PRAGUE SPRING
On my birthday, 30 April

A silent scream? The madrigal's top note?
Puking his wassail on the listening throng?
Mouthfuls of cumulus, then cobalt throat.
Medusa must have hexed him in mid-song.

The finest vantage point in all of Prague's
this gagging gargoyle's with the stone-locked lute,
leaning over cherries, blow-ups of Karl Marx
the pioneers 'll march past and salute.

Tomorrow's May but still a North wind scuffs
the plated surface like a maced cuirass,
lays on, lays off, gets purchase on and roughs
up the Vltava, then makes it glass.

The last snow of this year's late slow thaw
dribbles as spring saliva down his jaw.

Social Mobility

Ah, the proved advantages of scholarship!
Whereas his dad took cold tea for his snap,
he slaves at nuances, knows at just one sip
Château Lafite *from* Châteauneuf du Pape.

Heredity

How you became a poet's a mystery!
Wherever did you get your talent from?
I say: I had two uncles, Joe and Harry —
one was a stammerer, the other dumb.

On Not being Milton

For Sergio Vieira and Armando Guebuza (Frelimo)

Read and committed to the flames, I call
these sixteen lines that go back to my roots
my *Cahier d'un retour au pays natal*,
my growing black enough to fit my boots.

The stutter of the scold out of the branks
of condescension, class and counter-class
thickens with glottals to a lumpen mass
of Ludding morphemes closing up their ranks.
Each swung cast-iron Enoch of Leeds stress
clangs a forged music on the frames of Art,
the looms of owned language smashed apart!

Three cheers for mute ingloriousness!

Articulation is the tongue-tied's fighting.
In the silence round all poetry we quote
Tidd the Cato Street conspirator who wrote:

Sir, I Ham a very Bad Hand at Righting.

Note. An 'Enoch' is an iron sledge-hammer used by the Luddites to
smash the frames which were also made by the same Enoch Taylor
of Marsden. The cry was: 'Enoch made them, Enoch shall break
them!'

Classics Society

Leeds Grammar School 1552–1952

The grace of Tullies eloquence doth excell
any Englishmans tongue . . . my barbarous stile . . .

The tongue our leaders use to cast their spell
was once denounced as 'rude', 'gross', 'base' and 'vile'.

How fortunate we are who've come so far!

We boys can take old Hansards and translate
the British Empire into SPQR
but nothing demotic or too up to date,
and *not* the English that I speak at home,
not Hansard standards, and if Antoninus
spoke like delinquent Latin back in Rome
he'd probably get gamma double minus.

And so the lad who gets the alphas works
the hardest in his class at his translation
and finds good Ciceronian for Burke's:

a dreadful schism in the British nation.

National Trust

Bottomless pits. There's one in Castleton,
and stout upholders of our law and order
one day thought its depth worth wagering on
and borrowed a convict hush-hush from his warder
and winched him down; and back, flayed, grey, mad, dumb.

Not even a good flogging made him holler!

O gentlemen, a better way to plumb
the depths of Britain's dangling a scholar,
say, here at the booming shaft at Towanroath,
now National Trust, a place where they got tin,
those gentlemen who silenced the men's oath
and killed the language that they swore it in.

The dumb go down in history and disappear
and not one gentleman 's been brought to book:

Mes den hep tavas a-gollas y dyr

(Cornish) –

        'the tongueless man gets his land took.'

Continuous

James Cagney was the one up both our streets.
His was the only art we ever shared.
A gangster film and choc ice were the treats
that showed about as much love as he dared.

He'd be my own age now in '49!
The hand that glinted with the ring he wore,
his father's, tipped the cold bar into mine
just as the organist dropped through the floor.

He's on the platform lowered out of sight
to organ music, this time on looped tape,
into a furnace with a blinding light
where only his father's ring will keep its shape.

I wear it now to Cagneys on my own
and sense my father's hands cupped round my treat –

they feel as though they've been chilled to the bone
from holding my ice cream all through *White Heat*.

Marked with D.

When the chilled dough of his flesh went in an oven
not unlike those he fuelled all his life,
I thought of his cataracts ablaze with Heaven
and radiant with the sight of his dead wife,
light streaming from his mouth to shape her name,
'not Florence and not Flo but always Florrie'.
I thought how his cold tongue burst into flame
but only literally, which makes me sorry,
sorry for his sake there's no Heaven to reach.
I get it all from Earth my daily bread
but he hungered for release from mortal speech
that kept him down, the tongue that weighed like lead.

The baker's man that no one will see rise
and England made to feel like some dull oaf
is smoke, enough to sting one person's eyes
and ash (not unlike flour) for one small loaf.

Timer

Gold survives the fire that's hot enough
to make you ashes in a standard urn.
An envelope of coarse official buff
contains your wedding ring which wouldn't burn.

Dad told me I'd to tell them at St James's
that the ring should go in the incinerator.
That 'eternity' inscribed with both their names is
his surety that they'd be together, 'later'.

I signed for the parcelled clothing as the son,
the cardy, apron, pants, bra, dress —

the clerk phoned down: *6-8-8-3-1?*
Has she still her ring on? (Slight pause) *Yes!*

It's on my warm palm now, your burnished ring!

I feel your ashes, head, arms, breasts, womb, legs,
sift through its circle slowly, like that thing
you used to let me watch to time the eggs.

SONNETS FOR AUGUST 1945

1. THE MORNING AFTER

I

The fire left to itself might smoulder weeks.
Phone cables melt. Paint peels from off back gates.
Kitchen windows crack; the whole street reeks
of horsehair blazing. Still it celebrates.

Though people weep, their tears dry from the heat.
Faces flush with flame, beer, sheer relief
and such a sense of celebration in our street
for me it still means joy though banked with grief.

And that, now clouded, sense of public joy
with war-worn adults wild in their loud fling
has never come again since as a boy
I saw Leeds people dance and heard them sing.

There's still that dark, scorched circle on the road.
The morning after kids like me helped spray
hissing upholstery spring wire that still glowed
and cobbles boiling with black gas tar for V J.

II

The Rising Sun was blackened on those flames.
The jabbering tongues of fire consumed its rays.
Hiroshima, Nagasaki were mere names
for us small boys who gloried in our blaze.

The blood-red ball, first burnt to blackout shreds,
took hovering batwing on the bonfire's heat
above the *Rule Britannias* and the bobbing heads
of the V J hokey-cokey in our street.

The kitchen blackout cloth became a cloak
for me to play at fiend Count Dracula in.
I swirled it near the fire. It filled with smoke.
Heinz ketchup dribbled down my vampire's chin.

That circle of scorched cobbles scarred with tar 's
a night-sky globe nerve-rackingly all black,
both hemispheres entire but with no stars,
an Archerless zilch, a Scaleless zodiac.

2. OLD SOLDIER

Last years of Empire and the fifth of War
and *Camp* coffee extract on the kitchen table.
The Sikh that served the officer I saw
on the label in the label in the label
continuously cloned beyond my eyes,
beyond the range of any human staring,
down to amoeba, atom, neutron size,
but the turbaned bearer never lost his bearing
and nothing shook the bottle off his tray.
Through all infinity and down to almost zero
he holds out and can't die or fade away
loyal to the breakfasting Scots hero.

But since those two high summer days
the US dropped the World's first A-bombs on,
from that child's forever what returns my gaze
is a last chuprassie with all essence gone.

ART & EXTINCTION

'When I hear of the destruction of a species I feel as if all the works of some great writer had perished.'

— Theodore Roosevelt, 1899

1. THE BIRDS OF AMERICA

(I) John James Audubon (1785–1851)

The struggle to preserve once spoken words
from already too well-stuffed taxonomies
is a bit like Audubon's when painting birds,
whose method an admirer said was this:
Kill 'em, wire 'em, paint 'em, kill a fresh 'un!

The plumage even of the brightest faded.
The artist had to shoot in quick succession
till all the feathers were correctly shaded.

Birds don't pose for pictures when alive!
Audubon's idea of restraint,
doing the Pelican, was 25
dead specimens a day for *one* in paint.

By using them do we save words or not?

As much as Audubon's art could save a,
say, godwit, or a grackle, which he shot
and then saw 'multiplied by Havell's graver'.

(II) Weeki Wachee

Duds doomed to join the dodo: the dugong,
talonless eagles, croc, gimp manatee,
here, courtesy Creation's generous strong,
the losers of thinned jungle and slicked sea.

Many's the proud chieftain used to strut
round shady clearings of dark festooned teak
with twenty cockatoo tails on his nut,
macaw plumes à la mode, rainforest chic.

Such gladrag gaudies safe in quarantine
and spared at least their former jungle fate
of being blowpiped for vain primitives to preen
now race a tightrope on one roller skate.

A tanned sophomore, these ghettoed birds' Svengali,
shows glad teeth, evolved for smiling, as macaws
perform their deft Darwinian finale
by hoisting the Stars and Stripes for our applause.

(III) Standards

in hopeful anticipation of the bicentenary of the national emblem of
the United States of America, *Haliaaetus falco leucocephalus*, 1782–1982.

'The bald eagle is likewise a large, strong, and very active bird, but
an execrable tyrant: he supports his assumed dignity and grandeur by
rapine and violence, extorting unreasonable tribute and subsidy from
the feathered nations.'

– William Bartram, *Travels*, 1791

'Our standard with the eagle stands for us.
It waves in the breeze in almost every clime.'

(The flag, not *Falco leucocephalus*
poised in its dying on the brink of time!)

Rejecting Franklin's turkey for a bird that *flies*
Congress chose the soaring eagle, called,
for its conspicuous white head, 'the bald'.

Now the turkey's thriving and the eagle dies!

When the last stinks in its eyrie, or falls slow,
when the very last bald eagle goes the way
of all the unique fauna, it won't know
the Earth it plummets to 's the USA.

But will still wing over nations as the ghost
on money, and the mountainous US Post,

much as sunlight shining through the British pound
showed PEACE with her laurels, white on a green ground.

2. LOVING MEMORY
For Teresa Stratas

The fosses where Caractacus fought Rome
blend with grey bracken and become a blur
above the Swedish Nightingale's last home.

Somehow my need for you makes me seek her.

The Malverns darken as the dusk soaks in.
The rowan berries' dark red glaze grows dull.
The harvest moon's scraped silver and bruised tin
is only one night off from being full.

Death keeps all hours, but graveyards close at nights.
I hurry past the Malvern Hospital
where a nurse goes round small wards and puts on lights
and someone there's last night begins to fall.

'The oldest rocks this earth can boast', these hills,
packed with extinction, make me burn for you.

I ask two women leaving with dead daffodils:
Where's Jenny Lind's grave, please? They both say: *Who?*

3. LOOKING UP

For Philip, Terry and Will Sharpe and the bicentenary of the birth of
Peter Mark Roget (1779–1869)

All day till it grows dark I sit and stare
over Herefordshire hills and into Wales.
Reflections of red coals thrown on the air
blossom to brightness as the daylight fails.

An uncharred cherry flaunts a May of flames.
Like chaffinches and robins tongues of fire
flit with the burden of Creation's names
but find no new apostles to inspire.

Bar a farm house TV aerial or two,
the odd red bus, the red Post Office van,
this must have been exactly Roget's view,
good Dr Roget, the *Thesaurus* man.

Roget died here, but 90 when he died
of natural causes, twice as old as me.

Of his six synonyms for suicide
I set myself alight with safe suttee.

4. KILLING TIME

Among death-protected creatures in a case,
'The Earth's Endangered Species' on display
at a jam-packed terminal at JFK,
killing time again, I see my face
with Hawksbill Turtle, scrimshawed spermwhale bone,
the Margay of the family *Felidae*,
that, being threatened, cost the earth to buy.

And now with scientists about to clone
the long-haired mammoth back from Soviet frost,
my reflection's on the species the World's lost,
or will be losing in a little while,
which, as they near extinction, grow in worth,
the leopard, here a bag and matching purse,
the dancing shoes that were Nile crocodile,

the last *Felis pardalis* left on Earth,

the poet preserved beneath deep permaverse.

5. DARK TIMES

That the *Peppered Moth* was white and now is dark 's
a lesson in survival for Mankind.

Around the time Charles Darwin had declined
the dedication of *Das Kapital* by Marx
its predators could spot it on the soot,
but Industrial Revolution and Evolution taught
the moth to black its wings and not get caught
where all of Nature perished, or all but.

When lichens lighten some old smoke-grimed trees
and such as Yorkshire's millstacks now don't burn
and fish nose waters stagnant centuries,
can *Biston carbonaria* relearn,

if Man's awakened consciousness succeeds
in turning all these tides of blackness back
and diminishing the need for looking black,

to flutter white again above new Leeds?

6. t' ARK

Silence and poetry have their own reserves.
The numbered creatures flourish less and less.
A language near extinction best preserves
the deepest grammar of our nothingness.

Not only dodo, oryx and great auk
waddled on their tod to t'monster ark,
but 'leg', 'night', 'origin' in crushed people's talk,
tongues of fire last witnessed mouthing: *dark*!

Now when the future couldn't be much darker,
there being fewer epithets for sun,
and Cornish and the Togoland *Restsprache*
name both the animals and hunter's gun,
celebrate before things go too far
Papua's last reported manucode,
the pygmy hippo of the Côte d'Ivoire,
and Upper Guinea's oviparous toad –

(or mourn in Latin their imminent death,
then translate these poems into *cynghanedd*).

7. THE BIRDS OF JAPAN

Campi Phlegraei, Lake Nyos of Wum,
their sulphur could asphyxiate whole flocks
but combustibility had not yet come
to the femto-seconds of the *Fiat Nox*:
men made magma, flesh made fumaroles,
first mottled by the flash to brief mofettes
and Hiroshima's fast pressurizing souls
hissed through the fissures in mephitic jets.

Did the birds burst into song as they ignited
above billowing waves of cloud up in the sky,
hosannahs too short-lived to have alighted
on a Bomb-Age Bashō, or a Hokusai?

Apostles of that pinioned Pentecaust
of chirrupings cremated on the wing
will have to talk their ghosts down, or we're lost.
Until we know what they sang, who can sing?

8. THE POETRY LESSON

Its proboscis probes the basking monster's eye.
The *Flambeau*, whose ambrosia's salt dew
and nectars sucked from caymans' *lacrimae*,
survives on saurian secretions in Peru.

The blue fritillary of north Brazil
I saw uncurl the watchspring of its tongue
and, by syphoning or licking, have its fill
of goodnesses discarded in man's dung.
The question mark (complete with added dot)
crapped on the pavement in full public view
by cane-hooch-smashed emaciate was steaming hot
but ambrosia not shit to browsing Blue.

Both lessons in survival for fine words
to look for fodder where they've not yet looked –
be lepidoptera that browse on turds
or delicately drain the monster's duct.

A Kumquat for John Keats

Today I found the right fruit for my prime,
not orange, not tangelo, and not lime,
nor moon-like globes of grapefruit that now hang
outside our bedroom, nor tart lemon's tang
(though last year full of bile and self-defeat
I wanted to believe no life was sweet)
nor the tangible sunshine of the tangerine,
and no incongruous citrus ever seen
at greengrocers' in Newcastle or Leeds
misspelt by the spuds and mud-caked swedes,
a fruit an older poet might substitute
for the grape John Keats thought fit to be Joy's fruit,
when, two years before he died, he tried to write
how Melancholy dwelled inside Delight,
and if he'd known the citrus that I mean
that's not orange, lemon, lime or tangerine,
I'm pretty sure that Keats, though he had heard
'of candied apple, quince, and plum, and gourd'
instead of 'grape against the palate fine'
would have, if he'd known it, plumped for mine,
this Eastern citrus scarcely cherry size
he'd bite just once and then apostrophize
and pen one stanza how the fruit had all
the qualities of fruit before the Fall,
but in the next few lines be forced to write
how Eve's apple tasted at the second bite,
and if John Keats had only lived to be,
because of extra years, in need like me,
at 42 he'd help me celebrate
that Micanopy kumquat that I ate
whole, straight off the tree, sweet pulp and sour skin –
or was it sweet outside, and sour within?

For however many kumquats that I eat
I'm not sure if it's flesh or rind that's sweet,
and being a man of doubt at life's mid-way
I'd offer Keats some kumquats and I'd say:
You'll find that one part's sweet and one part's tart:
say where the sweetness or the sourness start.
I find I can't, as if one couldn't say
exactly where the night became the day,
which makes for me the kumquat taken whole
best fruit, and metaphor, to fit the soul
of one in Florida at 42 with Keats
crunching kumquats, thinking, as he eats
the flesh, the juice, the pith, the pips, the peel,
that this is how a full life ought to feel,
its perishable relish prick the tongue,
when the man who savours life 's no longer young,
the fruits that were his futures far behind.
Then it's the kumquat fruit expresses best
how days have darkness round them like a rind,
life has a skin of death that keeps its zest.

History, a life, the heart, the brain
flow to the taste buds and flow back again.
That decade or more past Keats's span
makes me an older not a wiser man,
who knows that it's too late for dying young,
but since youth leaves some sweetnesses unsung,
he's granted days and kumquats to express
Man's Being ripened by his Nothingness.
And it isn't just the gap of sixteen years,
a bigger crop of terrors, hopes and fears,
but a century of history on this earth
between John Keats's death and my own birth —
years like an open crater, gory, grim,
with bloody bubbles leering at the rim;

a thing no bigger than an urn explodes
and ravishes all silence, and all odes,
Flora asphyxiated by foul air
unknown to either Keats or Lemprière,
dehydrated Naiads, Dryad amputees
dragging themselves through slagscapes with no trees,
a shirt of Nessus fire that gnaws and eats
children half the age of dying Keats . . .

Now were you twenty five or six years old
when that fevered brow at last grew cold?
I've got no books to hand to check the dates.
My grudging but glad spirit celebrates
that all I've got to hand 's the kumquats, John,
the fruit I'd love to have your verdict on,
but dead men don't eat kumquats, or drink wine,
they shiver in the arms of Proserpine,
not warm in bed beside their Fanny Brawne,
nor watch her pick ripe grapefruit in the dawn
as I did, waking, when I saw her twist,
with one deft movement of a sunburnt wrist,
the moon, that feebly lit our last night's walk
past alligator swampland, off its stalk.
I thought of moon-juice juleps when I saw,
as if I'd never seen the moon before,
the planet glow among the fruit, and its pale light
make each citrus on the tree its satellite.

Each evening when I reach to draw the blind
stars seem the light zest squeezed through night's black rind;
the night's peeled fruit the sun, juiced of its rays,
first stains, then streaks, then floods the world with days,
days, when the very sunlight made me weep,
days, spent like the nights in deep, drugged sleep,
days in Newcastle by my daughter's bed,
wondering if she, or I, weren't better dead,

days in Leeds, grey days, my first dark suit,
my mother's wreaths stacked next to Christmas fruit,
and days, like this in Micanopy. Days!

As strong sun burns away the dawn's grey haze
I pick a kumquat and the branches spray
cold dew in my face to start the day.
The dawn's molasses make the citrus gleam
still in the orchards of the groves of dream.
The limes, like Galway after weeks of rain,
glow with a greenness that is close to pain,
the dew-cooled surfaces of fruit that spent
all last night flaming in the firmament.
The new day dawns. O days! My spirit greets
the kumquat with the spirit of John Keats.
O kumquat, comfort for not dying young,
both sweet and bitter, bless the poet's tongue!
I burst the whole fruit chilled by morning dew
against my palate. Fine, for 42!

I search for buzzards as the air grows clear
and see them ride fresh thermals overhead.
Their bleak cries were the first sound I could hear
when I stepped at the start of sunrise out of doors,
and a noise like last night's bedsprings on our bed
from Mr Fowler sharpening farmers' saws.

The Mother of the Muses

In memoriam Emmanuel Stratas, born Crete 1903, died Toronto 1987

After I've lit the fire and looked outside
and found us snowbound and the roads all blocked,
anxious to prove my memory's not ossified
and the way into that storehouse still unlocked,
as it's easier to remember poetry,
I try to remember, but soon find it hard,
a speech from *Prometheus* a boy from Greece BC
scratched, to help him learn it, on a shard.

I remember the museum, and I could eke
his scratch marks out, and could complete
the . . . however many lines there were of Greek
and didn't think it then much of a feat.
But now, not that much later, when I find
the verses I once knew beyond recall
I resolve to bring all yesterday to mind,
our visit to your father, each fact, *all*.

Seeing the Home he's in 's made me obsessed
with remembering those verses I once knew
and setting myself this little memory test
I don't think, at the moment, I'll come through.
It's the Memory, Mother of the Muses, bit.
Prometheus, in words I do recall reciting
but can't quote now, and they're so apposite,
claiming he gave Mankind the gift of writing,

along with fire the Gods withheld from men
who'd lived like ants in caves deprived of light
they could well end up living in again
if we let what flesh first roasted on ignite
a Burning of the Books far more extreme
than any screeching Führer could inspire,
the dark side of the proud Promethean dream
our globe enveloped in his gift of fire.

He bequeathed to baker and to bombardier,
to help benighted men develop faster,
two forms of fire, the gentle one in here,
and what the *Luftwaffe* unleashed, *and* the Lancaster.
One beneficial and one baleful form,
the fire I lit a while since in the grate
that's keeping me, as I sit writing, warm
and what gutted Goethestrasse on this date,

beginning yesterday to be precise
and shown on film from forty years ago
in a Home for the Aged almost glazed with ice
and surrounded by obliterating snow.
We had the choice of watching on TV
Dresden destroyed, then watching its rebirth,
or, with the world outside too blizzardful to see,
live, the senile not long for this earth.

Piles of cracked ice tiles where ploughs try to push
the muddied new falls onto shattered slates,
the glittering shrapnel of grey frozen slush,
a blitz debris fresh snow obliterates
along with what was cleared the day before
bringing even the snowploughs to a halt.
And their lives are frozen solid and won't thaw
with no memory to fling its sparks of salt.

The outer world of blur reflects their inner,
these Rest Home denizens who don't quite know
whether they've just had breakfast, lunch or dinner,
or stare, between three lunches, at the snow.
Long icicles from the low roof meet
the frozen drifts below and block their view
of flurry and blizzard in the snowed-up street
and of a sky that for a month has shown no blue.

Elsie's been her own optometrist,
measuring the daily way her sight declines
into a growing ball of flashing mist.
She trains her failing sight on outside signs:
the church's COME ALIVE IN '85!
the small hand on the *Export A* ad clock,
the flashing neon on the truck-stop dive
pulsing with strobe lights and jukebox rock,

the little red Scottie on the STOOP & SCOOP
but not the cute eye cast towards its rear,
the little rounded pile of heaped red poop
the owners are required to bend and clear.
To imagine herself so stooping is a feat
as hard as that of gymnasts she has seen
lissom in white leotards compete
in trampolining on the TV screen.

There's one with mashed dinner who can't summon
yet again the appetite to smear
the food about the shrunk face of a woman
weeping for death in her 92nd year.
And of the life she lived remembers little
and stares, like someone playing Kim's Game,
at the tray beneath her nose that fills with spittle
whose bubbles fill with faces with no name.

Lilian, whose love made her decide
to check in with her mate who'd had a stroke,
lost all her spryness once her husband died . . .
He had a beautiful . . . all made of oak . . .
silk inside . . . brass handles . . . tries to find
alternatives . . . *that long thing where you lie*
for words like coffin that have slipped her mind
and forgetting, not the funeral, makes her cry.

And Anne, who treats her roommates to her 'news'
though every day her news is just the same
how she'd just come back from *such a lovely cruise*
to that famous island . . . I forget its name . . .
Born before the Boer War, me, and so
I'm too old to remember I suppose . . .
then tries again . . . *the island's called . . . you know . . .*
that place, you know . . . where everybody goes . . .

First Gene had one and then a second cane
and then, in weeks, a walker of cold chrome,
now in a wheelchair wails for the Ukraine,
sobbing in soiled pants for what was home.
Is that horror at what's on the TV screen
or just the way the stroke makes Jock's jaw hang?
Though nobody quite knows what his words mean
they hear Scots diphthongs in the New World twang.

And like the Irish Sea on Blackpool Beach,
where Joan was once the pick of bathing belles,
the Lancashire she once had in her speech
seeps into Canadian as she retells,
whose legs now ooze out water, who can't walk,
how she was 'champion at tap', 'the flower'
(she poises the petals on the now frail stalk)
'of the ballet troupe at Blackpool Tower'.

You won't hear Gene, Eugene, Yevgeny speak
to nurses now, or God, in any other tongue
but his Ukrainian, nor your dad Greek,
all that's left to them of being young.
Life comes full circle when we die.
The circumference is finally complete,
so we shouldn't wonder too much why
his speech went back, a stowaway, to Crete.

Dispersal and displacement, willed or not,
from homeland to the room the three share here,
one Ukrainian, one Cretan, and one Scot
grow less Canadian as death draws near.
Jock sees a boozer in a Glasgow street,
and Eugene glittering icons, candles, prayer,
and for your dad a thorn-thick crag in Crete
with oregano and goat smells in the air.

And home? Where is it now? The olive grove
may well be levelled under folds of tar.
The wooden house made joyful with a stove
has gone the way of Tsar and samovar.
The small house with 8 people to a room
with no privacy for quiet thought or sex
bulldozed in the island's tourist boom
to make way for Big Macs and discothèques.

Beribboned hats and bold embroidered sashes
once helped another émigré forget
that Canada was going to get his ashes
and that Estonia's still Soviet.
But now the last of those old-timers
couldn't tell one folk dance from another
and mistakes in the mists of his Alzheimer's
the nurse who wipes his bottom for his mother.

Some hoard memories as some hoard gold
against that rapidly approaching day
that's all they have to live on, being old,
but find their savings spirited away.
What's the point of having lived at all
in the much-snapped duplex in Etobicoke
if it gets swept away beyond recall,
in spite of all the snapshots, at one stroke?

If we *are* what we remember, what are they
who don't have memories as we have ours,
who, when evening falls, have no recall of day,
or who those people were who'd brought them flowers.
The troubled conscience, though, 's glad to forget.
Oblivion for some 's an inner balm.
They've found some peace of mind, not total yet,
as only death itself brings that much calm.

And those white flashes on the TV screen,
as a child, whose dad plunged into genocide,
remembers Dresden and describes the scene,
are they from the firestorm then, or storm outside?
Crouching in clown's costume (it was *Fasching*)
aged, 40 years ago, as I was, 9
Eva remembers cellar ceiling crashing
and her mother screaming shrilly: *Swine! Swine! Swine!*

The Tiergarten chief with level voice remembered
a hippo disembowelled on its back,
a mother chimp, her charges all dismembered,
and trees bedaubed with zebra flesh and yak.
Flamingos, flocking from burst cages, fly
in a frenzy with their feathers all alight
from fire on the ground to bomb-crammed sky,
their flames fanned that much fiercer by their flight;

the gibbon with no hands he'd had to shoot
as it came towards him with appealing stumps,
the gutless gorilla still clutching fruit
mashed with its bowels into bloody lumps . . .
I was glad as on and on the keeper went
to the last flayed elephant's fire-frantic screech
that the old folk hadn't followed what was meant
by official footage or survivors' speech.

But then they missed the Semper's restoration,
Dresden's lauded effort to restore
one of the treasures of the now halved nation
exactly as it was before the War.
Billions of marks and years of labour
to reproduce the Semper and they play
what they'd played before the bombs fell, Weber,
Der Freischütz, for their reopening today.

Each bleb of blistered paintwork, every flake
of blast-flayed pigment in that dereliction
they analysed in lab flasks to remake
the colours needed for the redepiction
of Poetic Justice on her cloud surmounting
mortal suffering from opera and play,
repainted tales that seem to bear recounting
more often than the facts that mark today:

the dead Cordelia in the lap of Lear,
Lohengrin who pilots his white swan
at cascading lustres of bright chandelier
above the plush this pantheon shattered on,
with Titania's leashed pards in pastiche Titian,
Faust with Mephisto, Joan, Nathan the Wise,
all were blown, on that Allied bombing mission,
out of their painted clouds into the skies.

Repainted, reupholstered, all in place
just as it had been before that fatal night,
but however devilish the leading bass
his demons are outshadowed on this site.
But that's what Dresden wants and so they play
the same score sung by new uplifting voices
and, as opera synopses often say,
'The curtain falls as everyone rejoices.'

Next more TV, devoted to the trial
of Ernst Zundel, who denies the Jews were gassed,
and academics are supporting his denial,
restoring pride by doctoring the past,
and not just Germans but those people who
can't bear to think such things could ever be,
and by disbelieving horrors to be true
hope to put back hope in history.

A nurse comes in to offer us a cot
considering how bad the blizzard's grown
but you kissed your dad, who, as we left, forgot
he'd been anything all day but on his own.
We needed to escape, weep, laugh, and lie
in each other's arms more privately than there,
weigh in the balance all we're heartened by,
so braved the blizzard back, deep in despair.

Feet of snow went sliding off the bonnet
as we pulled onto the road from where we'd parked.
A snowplough tried to help us to stay on it
but localities nearby, once clearly marked,
those named for northern hometowns close to mine,
the Yorks, the Whitbys and the Scarboroughs,
all seemed one whited-out recurring sign
that could well be 'Where everybody goes . . .'

His goggles bug-eyed from the driven snow,
the balaclavaed salter goes ahead
with half the sower's, half the sandman's throw,
and follows the groaning plough with wary tread.
We keep on losing the blue revolving light
and the sliding salter, and try to keep on track
by making sure we always have in sight
the yellow Day-glo X marked on his back.

The blizzard made our neighbourhood unknown.
We could neither see behind us nor before.
We felt in the white-out world we were alone
looking for landmarks, lost, until we saw
the unmistakable McDonald's M
with its '60 billion served' hamburger count.
Living, we were numbered among them,
and dead, among an incomputable amount . . .

I woke long after noon with you still sleeping
and the windows blocked where all the snow had blown.
Your pillow was still damp from last night's weeping.
In that silent dark I swore I'd make it known,
while the oil of memory feeds the wick of life
and the flame from it's still constant and still bright,
that, come oblivion or not, I loved my wife
in that long thing where we lay with day like night.

Toronto's at a standstill under snow.
Outside there's not much light and not a sound.
Those lines from Aeschylus! How do they go?
It's almost halfway through *Prometheus Bound*.
I think they're coming back. I'm concentrating . . .
μουσομητορ 'εργανην . . . Damn! I forget,
but remembering your dad, I'm celebrating
being in love, not too forgetful, yet.

Country people used to say today's
the day the birds sense spring and choose their mates,
and trapped exotics in the Dresden blaze
were flung together in their flame-fledged fates.
The snow in the street outside 's at least 6ft.
I look for life, and find the only sign 's,
like words left for, or *by*, someone from Crete,
a bird's tracks, like blurred Greek, for Valentine's.

Toronto,
St Valentine's Day

Initial Illumination

Farne cormorants with catches in their beaks
shower fishscale confetti on the shining sea.
The first bright weather here for many weeks
for my Sunday G-Day train bound for Dundee,
off to St Andrews to record a reading,
doubtful, in these dark days, what poems can do,
and watching the mists round Lindisfarne receding
my doubt extends to Dark Age Good Book too.
Eadfrith the Saxon scribe/illuminator
incorporated cormorants I'm seeing fly
round the same island thirteen centuries later
into the *In principio*'s initial I.
Billfrith's begemmed and jewelled boards got looted
by raiders gung-ho for booty and berserk,
the sort of soldiery that's still recruited
to do today's dictators' dirty work,
but the initials in St John and in St Mark
graced with local cormorants in ages,
we of a darker still keep calling Dark,
survive in those illuminated pages.
The word of God so beautifully scripted
by Eadfrith and Billfrith the anchorite
Pentagon conners have once again conscripted
to gloss the cross on the precision sight.
Candlepower, steady hand, gold leaf, a brush
were all that Eadfrith had to beautify
the word of God much bandied by George Bush
whose word illuminated midnight sky
and confused the Baghdad cock who was betrayed
by bombs into believing day was dawning
and crowed his heart out at the deadly raid
and didn't live to greet the proper morning.

Now with noonday headlights in Kuwait
and the burial of the blackened in Baghdad
let them remember, all those who celebrate,
that their good news is someone else's bad
or the light will never dawn on poor Mankind.
Is it open-armed at all that Victory V,
that insular initial intertwined
with slack-necked cormorants from black laquered sea,
with trumpets bulled and bellicose and blowing
for what men claim as victories in their wars,
with the fire-hailing cock and all those crowing
who don't yet smell the dunghill at their claws?

Acknowledgements

The poems in this selection are taken from the following books, to whose publishers acknowledgement is made: *Zoom!* (Bloodaxe, 1989), *Kid* (Faber and Faber, 1992) and *Book of Matches* (Faber and Faber, 1993) by Simon Armitage; *The Indoor Park* (Bloodaxe, 1983), *The Frighteners* (Bloodaxe, 1987), *HMS Glasshouse* (Oxford University Press, 1991) and *Ghost Train* (Oxford University Press, 1995) by Sean O'Brien; *The Loiners* (London Magazine Editions, 1970), *The School of Eloquence* (Rex Collings Ltd, 1978), *Continuous* (Rex Collings Ltd, 1981), *A Kumquat for John Keats* (Bloodaxe, 1981), *Ten Sonnets from the School of Eloquence* (Anvil Press, 1987), *Selected Poems* (Penguin, second edition 1987), *Tony Harrison: Bloodaxe Critical Anthologies* (Bloodaxe, 1991) and *The Gaze of the Gorgon* (Bloodaxe, 1992) by Tony Harrison.